The ACE BASIN

A Lowcountry Legacy

PETE LAURIE

Photography by Phillip Jones

THE
History
PRESS

Published by The History Press
Charleston, SC 29403
www.historypress.net

Copyright © 2015 by Pete Laurie
All rights reserved

First published 2015

Manufactured in the United States

ISBN 978.1.62619.776.3

Library of Congress Control Number: 2015945060

CONTENTS

1. History of the ACE Basin Project   7
2. ACE Basin Habitats   15
3. The Seasons   27

Bibliography   151
Index   153
About the Author and Photographer   159

The ACE Basin core area covers 350,000 acres in southeastern South Carolina.
South Carolina Department of Natural Resources.

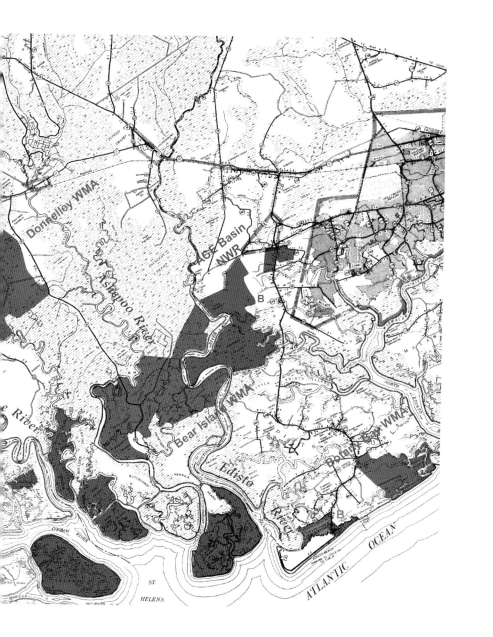

1

HISTORY OF THE ACE BASIN PROJECT

As the early rice planters diked off thousands of acres of wetlands along the Ashepoo, Combahee and Edisto Rivers and cleared them of timber, they had no idea that the resulting habitat would one day become a mecca for migrating waterfowl. Nor could they have anticipated the Industrial Revolution of the eighteenth and nineteenth centuries that generated a wealthy upper class, a portion of which would develop a passion for waterfowl hunting. When the once highly profitable rice culture collapsed shortly after 1900 from a variety of pressures, mostly economic, the rice fields, built and maintained at great cost for over 150 years, might have gradually reverted back to natural wetlands had wealthy northerners not bought up the old plantations. These new owners had the interest and the capital to repair and restore the crumbling dikes, not for profit, but for sport. Many of these new owners continued to live in northern states but came south every fall and winter to hunt ducks, as well as quail and deer. Most had the resources to maintain these properties at a high level and to resist the development pressures that overwhelmed many natural areas in Charleston to the north and Beaufort to the south.

While no longer "pristine" after centuries of agriculture, timber harvest, construction of impoundments and other activities, this large section of the South Carolina coastal plain has largely been spared commercial and residential development. The region's three winding rivers and associated wetlands have greatly impeded land transportation over the years, and even today, very few roads allow access to most of lower Colleton County and

Seen from the air, old rice fields, now managed for wintering waterfowl, line the upper Combahee River. *Phillip Jones.*

surrounding sections of Beaufort and Charleston Counties. By the 1980s, this area, which U.S. Fish and Wildlife Service biologist Nora Murdock first dubbed the "ACE Basin," had become a natural oasis on the state's rapidly developing coast. But would succeeding generations keep these large properties intact and undeveloped, especially as waterfowl populations declined and fewer young people retained a passion for sport hunting?

In 1986, using funds available through Ducks Unlimited, a national conservation organization made up primarily of waterfowl hunters, the State of South Carolina purchased Springfield Marsh, 696 acres of wetlands along the South Edisto River. The owners, a hunting club from Columbia, did not want to spend the money to repair failing dikes that threatened to render the area much less attractive to wintering waterfowl. Biologists with the state wildlife department, now the South Carolina Department of Natural Resources (DNR), saw an opportunity to enhance the adjacent Bear Island Wildlife Management Area (WMA) by adding freshwater impoundments to its mostly brackish wetlands, thus increasing the variety of ducks the area could attract for public waterfowl hunting. Ducks Unlimited wanted to preserve good waterfowl habitat and had the funds to purchase the land but not the staff to manage it. In the end, everyone won: the original owners made a profit on the sale of the land, Ducks Unlimited protected waterfowl habitat, the state got a valuable addition to its game lands and it cost the taxpayer nothing.

A year later, in a similar arrangement, Gaylord and Dorothy Donnelley donated Sampson Island, 100 acres of upland and 2,600 acres of tidal marsh to The Nature Conservancy (TNC), which then transferred it to the state as another addition to Bear Island WMA. These two very successful partnerships among private landowners, a conservation organization and the state government caught the eye of a number of people interested in preserving the status quo in the ACE Basin.

The early project visionaries knew that to ensure success, they had to have the full cooperation of three often competing entities: government agencies (both state and federal), conservation organizations and, most importantly, private landowners. So they put together a grass-roots organization of individuals, all having the same agenda and mutual respect for one another, and called it the ACE Basin Task Force. The task force set up the ACE Basin Project with an area of 350,000 acres and a goal to eventually protect 90,000 acres within that area. Having already donated Sampson Island to TNC, Gaylord Donnelley, a nationally recognized conservationist and owner of Ashepoo Plantation, quickly provided support and later, through conservation easements and land donations, helped protect thousands of additional acres. From the beginning, Donnelley, who owned a Chicago publishing empire, saw the importance of protecting the entire area not just by piecemeal efforts but through a "Grand Vision," as it became known. Other early conservation easements by key landowners, such as Hugh Lane Sr. and Ted Turner, inspired neighboring property owners, who quickly realized that conservation easements on their properties offered real advantages.

Through a conservation easement, a property owner agrees to restrict the type and amount of development that may take place on his property and conveys the right to enforce these restrictions to a qualified conservation organization. Should the property change hands, the conservation easement goes right along with the deed, and the new owner must abide by the same restrictions. Tailored to the particular interests of the property owner, conservation easements in the ACE Basin typically allow traditional uses, such as timber management, hunting and fishing, but greatly restrict commercial or residential development. Because many of the landholdings within the ACE include thousands of acres, a single conservation easement protects a large area, without cost to the taxpayer to purchase or maintain the property. While these lands remain private property, the public at large

The sale of forest products helps fund the maintenance of both public and private lands within the ACE, providing a renewable source of income to landowners. *Phillip Jones.*

benefits indirectly from the conservation and protection of natural areas and vital wildlife habitat.

The ACE Basin Project got another boost in 1990, when the U.S. Fish and Wildlife Service established the ACE Basin National Wildlife Refuge with the purchase of the 832-acre Bonny Hall Club on the Combahee River. The following year, TNC helped the Fish and Wildlife Service add to the refuge with the purchase of the Grove Plantation on the Edisto River in Charleston County. The antebellum house there became the refuge headquarters. Instrumental in securing funds for refuge land purchases, including Bonny Hall Plantation as an addition to the new refuge, Senator Fritz Hollings said in 1992, "The ACE Basin is nationally recognized as a unique natural resource area, and I am committed to its protection." In recognition of his support in establishing the refuge, the U.S. Fish and Wildlife Service eventually renamed it the "Ernest F. Hollings ACE Basin National Wildlife Refuge."

By 1991, the ACE Basin Project had protected more than 40,000 acres, including the 12,500-acre Cheeha-Combahee Plantation, a key property in southeastern Colleton County.

With much of the project area consisting of salt marsh and estuarine waters, planners from the beginning wanted to buy into a federal program designed to protect the nation's many key estuarine ecosystems. St. Helena

The Grove Plantation house serves as headquarters for the Hollings National Wildlife Refuge on the Edisto River. *Pete Laurie.*

Sound, bordered by hundreds of acres of marsh dotted with small, uninhabited islands, fit right into the National Estuarine Research Reserve (NERR) system. With Senator Hollings again providing the funding, the state established the ACE Basin NERR, managed by the Department of Natural Resources, with a core of 14,000 acres, including Ashe, Beet, Big, Warren, South Williman and Buzzard Islands, along with surrounding marshes. Later acquisitions to the NERR included Pine, Otter and Morgan Islands. The purchase of Morgan Island prevented a purported $40 million development that would have placed sixty-four houses on the 4,489-acre island in the heart of the NERR.

The NERR program provides annual funding for research and educational activities, coordinated through the DNR. Educational groups, from public schools to colleges and universities, can tour the area and participate in special on-site programs. With federal funding through the NERR, DNR educators began taking school groups on half-day cruises into the marsh creeks and St. Helena Sound on research vessels, a program that has increased in popularity and expanded to include adult groups.

In 1992, the South Carolina Department of Natural Resources assumed management of the formerly private eight-thousand-acre Mary's Island

Plantation through a complex set of transactions involving Ducks Unlimited, the U.S. Army Corps of Engineers, the National Wild Turkey Federation and other organizations. The agency named the property "Donnelley Wildlife Management Area" in honor of the pioneering conservation efforts of Gaylord Donnelley (who had died a year earlier) and his wife, Dorothy. This acquisition protected a key property bordering both U.S. Highway 17 and Bennetts Point Road. In 1993, Dorothy Donnelley granted conservation easements on Ashepoo Plantation and Fenwick Island, adding two more key properties to the project area.

Success continued to build on success in 1995 as Eugene DuPont willed his 9,800-acre Nemours Plantation to the nonprofit Nemours Plantation Wildlife Foundation, securing a historic rice plantation on the Beaufort County side of the Combahee River. DuPont also provided perpetual funding for the foundation to conduct wildlife research on Nemours. In 1996, an easement on Lavington Plantation completed a 22,000-acre corridor of protection from the Combahee River to the Ashepoo River.

By 1998, just ten years after its formation, through land purchases from willing sellers by state and federal agencies and through easements to conservation organizations, the ACE Basin Project had protected an amazing 128,000 acres, far surpassing the initial goal of 90,000 acres set in

Hardwood forests line the extensive drainage of the upper Edisto River. *Pete Laurie.*

1990. In 2002, MeadWestvaco, which had supported the project for years, sold a conservation easement to the DNR that protected 5,800 acres along the Edisto River between Highway 17A and Highway 17. Protecting this stretch of the river from development helped to maintain water quality throughout the basin.

A year later, the DNR completed the NERR Field Station at Bennett's Point and dedicated it to Michael D. McKenzie, who served as the NERR's first manager and played a key role in securing early funding to acquire properties in the reserve as well as establishing the framework for research and educational programs. The 4,100-square-foot facility contains labs, a meeting room and a dormitory to accommodate visiting scientists, managers, educators and students.

In 2006, recognizing the importance of protecting the entire watershed to ensure water quality throughout the basin, the ACE Basin Task Force expanded the project to encompass one million acres extending to Orangeburg on the upper reaches of the Edisto, by far the longest of the three rivers. Within this expanded area, Norfolk Southern Railroad quickly donated a conservation easement on 12,488 acres of the Brosnan Forest to the Lowcountry Open Land Trust, one of the largest single easements in state history.

Live oaks arch across the main road at Botany Bay Plantation on a foggy morning. *Phillip Jones.*

In 2008, the DNR received another vital property that for decades had been in private ownership and off limits to the public when Botany Bay Plantation became state property through an earlier deed agreement after the death of owner Margaret Pepper. This 4,630-acre property on Edisto Island includes an easily accessible front beach, one of the few in the project area. Protecting the southeast corner of the ACE Basin and in an area of considerable tourist traffic, Botany Bay immediately received an influx of public use, attracting fifty thousand visitors in its first year.

The ACE Basin Project has now protected well over 200,000 acres, far beyond initial goals and expectations, and has become one of the most successful land preservation efforts in the country. The unique partnership of state and federal agencies, conservation organizations and private landowners has become a model of other land protection efforts throughout the country. The project includes 70,000 acres of public lands and more than 150 conservation easements on private lands.

2

ACE BASIN HABITATS

The core area of the ACE Basin consists of 350,000 acres in the lower drainages of the Ashepoo, Combahee and Edisto Rivers on the southern coast of South Carolina. Wetlands make up about half of this total area, with 91,000 acres of tidal wetlands, 55,000 acres of forested wetlands and 26,000 acres of managed wetlands (impoundments). This large amount of wetlands of several types makes the ACE Basin ideal habitat for myriad plants and animals. These wetlands also have impeded human access and thus protected the area from industrial and residential development. However, centuries of habitat alteration and manipulation to grow crops—including indigo, rice and cotton—as well as forest products, such as timber and pulpwood, have left the entire area, wetlands and uplands, far from pristine. In 2006, the ACE Basin Task Force expanded the ACE Basin Project Area to encompass 1 million acres extending well up the Edisto River. This book, however, covers primarily the original core area.

FRONT BEACH

The ACE Basin contains four front beaches—Botany Bay, Edisto Beach, Otter Island and Hunting Island State Park—all of them accessible to the public. While together they make up only a small fraction of the basin's landmass, beaches add a unique dimension to the area. Beaches in the ACE

Rapid and continuous change limits diversity on the intertidal beach, which serves as a transition zone between ocean and land. *Phillip Jones.*

have little slope and a wide expanse at low tide. Severe erosion in many areas has obliterated the dune field of the upper beach, pushing the waves into the adjacent maritime forest or into the salt marsh behind the beach. Lacking dunes, these beaches consists of the intertidal zone, flooded during twice-daily high tides, and the nearshore subtidal zone.

On the intertidal beach a variety of microscopic algae thrive among the sand grains while larger attached or floating algae grow below the low tide mark where storms may wash them onto the beach. Above the high tide mark, a few hardy emergent plants, such as sea oats, silver croton and panic grass, manage to survive the harsh conditions of wind, salt spray and poor soils. The transition zone, between the beach and inland habitats, supports a few flowering plants and hardy trees and shrubs, including cabbage palmetto and live oak.

The intertidal beach, with its sudden and continual changes from wet to dry and hot to cold, limits the diversity of beach fauna. Most beach residents remain permanently buried and out of reach of predators or have the ability to quickly bury themselves when left high and dry by the retreating tide. A variety of marine worms live below the beach surface, filtering food particles from the incoming tide. Several species of small clams wash inland on the incoming tide, dig into the sand and then siphon organic matter from the water column. On the falling tide, they retreat, staying underwater throughout the tidal cycle. Marine snails of many types live just offshore from the beach, and while the snails have short lifespans, their calcified shells often wash onto the beach and can endure for many years. A few crustaceans, such as mole crabs, hermit crabs and ghost shrimp, also manage to survive in the dynamic intertidal zone. Horseshoe crabs invade some beaches in large numbers each spring to lay eggs, an important source of food for migrating shorebirds, especially red knots.

Predatory fishes of the surf zone take advantage of the incoming tides to move onto the beach to feed on the invertebrates living there. These fishes include flounder, spot, bluefish and red drum, along with several species of sharks. Many species of shorebirds, most of them migratory, feed or rest on ACE Basin beaches, as do terns and gulls. Marine turtles, primarily the loggerhead, nest on these beaches in spring and summer.

ESTUARY

The three rivers of the ACE Basin converge into St. Helena Sound, although part of the Edisto, referred to as the North Edisto, splits off at the Dawhoo River and travels a separate route, entering the Atlantic Ocean farther north. In addition, several other small rivers—the Coosaw, the Morgan and the Harbor—add to the sound's waters from the south. The freshwater flow these rivers bring from inland mixes with the salty

Estuaries, among the world's most productive habitats, form where the fresh water of rivers mixes with salt water pushed inland by ocean tides. *Phillip Jones.*

waters of the Atlantic, which has free access to the sound on the east across the seven-mile gap between Edisto Island to the north and Hunting Island to the south.

Estuaries formed at the mouths of larger rivers, such as the Santee, develop a salt wedge as the lighter fresh water of the river rides over the denser salt water coming in from the ocean. However, the relatively small influx of fresh water from the smaller ACE Basin rivers allows fresh and salt water to mix without forming a salt wedge. This mixing generates constantly changing patterns of salinity and temperatures. Water circulation varies with the height of the twice-daily tides, wind direction and velocity and the amount of rainfall. Strong easterly winds can push a normal high tide much higher while a westerly wind can impede the influx of salt water at high tide.

In this dynamic environment, nutrients flushed downstream from inland areas and well circulated by currents generated by the constant rise and fall of the tide make estuaries among the most productive of all habitats. Primary production from algae provides dissolved oxygen through photosynthesis by both phytoplankton and macro-algae, such as sea lettuce.

To survive in such an unstable environment, animals must have a high tolerance for rapid changes in temperature and salinity or have the mobility to move away from unsuitable conditions. Mud flats support high concentrations of invertebrates, providing excellent foraging areas for birds during low water and for aquatic predators when inundated by the tides. Oyster beds provide habitat for shrimp, crabs and many species of small fishes. Fish species include herbivores, such as mullet and menhaden, as well as predators, including red drum, spotted seatrout, flounder and many others. Bottlenose dolphins forage throughout estuaries.

SALT MARSH

The ACE Basin's extensive salt marshes and the meandering creeks that alternately flood and drain these grasslands serve as a transition zone between the estuary and uplands. Salinity in salt marshes ranges from near zero to the strength of seawater, depending on the height of the tides and the amount of rainfall. As the reach of ocean water diminishes with elevation, salt marshes bordering tidal rivers gradually become brackish marshes and finally freshwater marshes but remain tidal as far as thirty miles inland.

Salt marshes and their meandering creeks serve as a transition zone between estuaries and uplands. *Pete Laurie.*

The twice-daily inundation of salt water into the marsh creates a hostile environment for most plants. However, salt marsh cord grass, also known as spartina, thrives under these harsh conditions, occurring in wide expanses of virtually pure stands, tall and luxuriant along the well-flushed creek banks but much shorter in the upper marsh. In areas with just a few additional inches of elevation, a handful of other plants, notably black needle rush, replace spartina. With ample nutrients supplied by the incoming rivers and circulated by the tides and currents, combined with abundant sunlight, these marshes provide primary production to the estuary. As the considerable annual production of marsh plants dies back to the roots each winter, bacteria gradually break it down into detritus. These small food particles become available to the many juvenile fishes and invertebrates that use salt marshes as nursery areas. The constantly changing salt marsh environment greatly limits resident fauna to a few highly tolerant species, notably fiddler crabs, marsh crabs, periwinkles, ribbed mussels, oysters and clams.

Freshwater Marsh

Inland from the immediate coast and the St. Helena Sound estuary, salt marshes gradually become brackish and eventually change into freshwater marshes. Salinity and how far it extends upriver varies greatly with the height of the tide and the amount of freshwater flow from rainfall farther inland. Since fishing regulations vary from salt water to fresh, the DNR has established arbitrary freshwater/saltwater lines on major coastal streams strictly for law enforcement purposes. Well above the reach of salt water, water levels rise and fall with the tides as far as thirty miles inland. Without the limiting effect of salt, these wetlands support one of the most diverse plant communities in the country. While some brackish marsh plants inhabit these tidal marshes, freshwater species, such as giant cutgrass, maidencane and many others, dominate.

Freshwater wetlands include not only emergent plants but also shrubs, such as buttonbush and swamp rose. In some areas, these wetlands develop into wooded swamps consisting of bald cypress, water tupelo, red maple and other trees. Rice planters cleared thousands of acres of

ACE Basin freshwater wetlands, some of them tidal, include old rice fields that have reverted back to original plant communities. *Pete Laurie.*

this habitat, converting it into shallow, diked fields for rice cultivation. Since the demise of the rice culture in this area one hundred years ago, some former rice fields have reverted back to a resemblance of their original plant communities.

IMPOUNDMENTS

Most of the ACE Basin's impoundments, also referred to as managed wetlands, can trace their origins to the rice culture that began in South Carolina about 1694. Rice planters diked off sections along the edges of coastal rivers and streams, cleared the native vegetation and planted rice in fields where they could manipulate water levels using the rise and fall of the tide. When the state's rice culture eventually collapsed just after the turn of the twentieth century, wealthy northern industrialists bought up the defunct rice plantations and began managing them to attract wintering waterfowl for sport hunting. The ACE Basin core currently contains twenty-six thousand acres of impoundments, a small percentage of the area but a key habitat for many plants and animals and one of the most intensely managed.

Most waterfowl impoundments in the ACE Basin once served as rice fields. *Pete Laurie.*

Using water control structures called trunks, property managers can carefully raise or lower water levels in these shallow ponds that range from fewer than twenty acres to more than five hundred. Instead of growing the once lucrative Carolina Gold rice, today's managers encourage the growth of native waterfowl plants, such as widgeon grass, dwarf spike rush and salt marsh bulrush. These plants grow best in brackish water, with most impoundments maintained at a salinity of five to twenty-five parts per thousand. In impoundments with only fresh water available, management practices encourage red root and panic grass, favorites of many duck species. Other plants that inhabit impoundments range from cord grass and black needle rush in high salinity impoundments to saw grass and cattails in brackish areas and pickerelweed, frog-bit and even red maple and bald cypress in freshwater impoundments.

Management practices may include planting corn and other grain in ponds where, when drained, the substrate will support mechanized equipment. Burning native vegetation in the fall and then flooding the fields makes seeds more readily available to waterfowl.

Impoundments also provide ideal habitat for many species other than waterfowl. Depending on water levels, wading birds, such as herons, egrets and ibises, along with migrating shorebirds feed on the myriad small fishes and invertebrates that become trapped in impoundments. Ospreys and bald eagles also feed in impoundments, and alligators find ideal habitat in the warm, shallow waters. Mink, otters and raccoons all forage in impoundments, and white-tailed deer sometimes graze where the substrate will support their sharp hooves.

FORESTED WETLANDS

The majority of the ACE Basin's fifty-five thousand acres of forested wetlands occurs in the Salkehatchie Swamp, which extends from Yemasee up the Salkehatchie River to South Carolina Highway 63. Other forested wetlands in the basin exist along the upper reaches of the three rivers and in smaller, isolated areas, such as Tupelo Pond on Donnelley WMA.

River swamps develop along the slowly flowing and meandering streams where regular flooding spills water out of the banks and into the surrounding forest. Floodwaters gradually seep back into the main channel, delaying sudden damaging floods and drastic changes in salinity farther

Forested wetlands occur along the upper reaches of the three rivers and in isolated low areas, such as Tupelo Pond on Donnelley WMA. *Phillip Jones.*

downstream. However, this regular inundation of the surrounding forest produces saturated soils with little oxygen. Trees in this habitat generally have shallow root systems, adapted to absorb some oxygen from the air, as well as buttressed trunks and other adaptations, such as cypress knees. Common tree species include bald cypress, water tupelo, red maple, sweet gum, black gum and red cedar. The inability to withstand regular flooding limits understory plants, and plant communities vary with only slight changes in elevation and subsequent frequency and duration of flooding. Common plants of these wetlands include lizard tail, pickerelweed, arrowhead and swamp dock.

Swamp invertebrates, including insects, isopods, amphipods, worms, snails and clams, often occur in very high densities based on constantly changing physical conditions of flood and drought. The wide flood plain offers nursery areas for riverine fishes, including bream of several species, redfin pickerel, longnose gar, mudfish, largemouth bass and several species of catfish. Anadramous species, such as American shad, blueback herring and Atlantic sturgeon, spawn in these wetlands each spring. Snakes, turtles and a great variety of frogs and salamanders also utilize forested wetlands, as do many resident and migrant birds and a number of mammals.

UPLANDS

Uplands make up about half of the ACE Basin's core area of 350,000 acres. Scattered and fragmented by an almost equal acreage of wetlands of various types, much of these uplands have limited overland access. This difficulty of access has historically restricted both residential and commercial development. Upland habitats include old field, pine forest, mixed pine-hardwoods and mixed hardwood forest. Far from pristine, uplands within the basin have produced timber and pulpwood for decades and, before that, cotton and indigo. Areas managed for timber and pulpwood undergo regular burning to control the growth of understory hardwoods and halt natural plant succession. Pines—mostly loblolly and slash, along with some longleaf—dominate the higher sandy ridges, giving way to oaks, hickories and other hardwoods in the slightly lower elevations. Mixed pine-hardwood stands occur throughout. Many property owners plant a portion of their lands annually with corn, sunflowers and other grains primarily for the benefit of deer, doves and other game and nongame species. Revenue from

Uplands include forested areas managed for timber and pulpwood where controlled burning limits the growth of understory hardwoods. *Pete Laurie.*

the harvest of forest products and from the leasing of uplands to hunt clubs helps large landowners pay property taxes and maintenance costs.

Maritime forests develop on barrier islands and on inland areas close to tidal marshes or front beaches. The ACE Basin contains about five hundred acres of maritime forest, most of it on Otter, Pine and South Fenwick Islands within the National Estuarine Research Reserve. These forests consist of live oak, laurel oak, red bay, American holly, southern magnolia, red cedar, cabbage palmetto, yaupon holly and wax myrtle. These mostly evergreen species shed leaves throughout the year, providing continual nutrients to the poor, sandy soil. Maritime forests provide critical habitat for many migrating species of song birds, as well as small mammals, reptiles and amphibians. Outside the ACE Basin, residential and resort development along the coast has altered or destroyed many of the state's original maritime forests.

3

THE SEASONS

Spring

Spring got a late start in the ACE Basin as a cold, miserable February lingered into a dismal first week of March. Finally, on a sunny morning at Donnelley Wildlife Management Area, I noted the first signs of spring slowly emerging. The temperature remained in the forties, but both plants and animals had begun to respond to the lengthening days of early spring. Along the swamp edges, winged seeds of red maples drooped in rusty red clusters. In the uplands, loblolly pines bristled with yellow-green buds about to erupt into clouds of pollen, and the tips of southern red oaks hung with small, wrinkled new leaves and dangling beads of green flowers stirred by the breeze. In the understory, the tops of devil's walking sticks sprouted little fountains of new green leaves. Live oak leaves that had remained green all winter turned brown and dropped from the spreading branches, replaced as they fell with new lighter-green spring foliage, keeping the trees perennially green and "live" throughout the seasons.

The spring morning brought familiar sounds as well. A male rufous-sided towhee sang, "Drink your tea," over and over from the top of a small sweet gum, its bare branches tipped with green leaf buds. The relentless "chee, chee, chee" of yellow-throated warblers and the jumbled little song of white-eyed vireos filled the woodlands against a background medley of cardinals and Carolina wrens, all tuning up to stake out nesting territories. In the distance, woodpeckers of several species kept up a steady drumbeat on hollow tree limbs. Red-winged blackbirds seemed caught between the seasons. A few males had taken up residence in the freshwater marshes, alerting rivals with their "conk-a-ree" song of spring. But I also heard a chattering winter-like flock of redwings, containing both sexes, at the top of a sweet gum, where they picked at the fat green buds. A winter holdover orange-crowned warbler, bright yellow-green in the morning sun and apparently not yet ready to migrate north, foraged among a clump of switch cane at the edge of a plowed field. And everywhere the excess water from weeks of winter rain poured from the woods in narrow, twisting drains that snaked their way toward the old rice field complex, where at low tide, the runoff surged through open trunks and into the Chehaw River.

But despite any lingering remnants of winter, spring prevailed. Wood ducks now flushed from the flooded trees in pairs, not flocks, while the jumbled chuckle of breeding leopard frogs rose from grassy low spots. In a flock of soon-to-depart yellow-rumped warblers, one male had already molted into the brighter plumage of spring. A flock of about fifty ring-necked ducks, scarce all winter, paddled about on an old rice field reserve, enjoying a short break on their northward journey. An immature little blue heron, still white and awaiting its adult plumage, stalked among the lily pads. As the day warmed, two eight-foot alligators crawled onto a causeway to bask in the spring sun. I drove within six feet of them before they reluctantly splashed back into the still chilly water. By midday, yellow-bellied sliders, the common freshwater turtle of the ACE Basin, had also hauled out to bask on any sunlit bank or fallen log, and a large banded water snake slid quickly across the sandy road that split a marshy area. Later, I noticed a yellow rat snake about ten feet up a big pecan tree. As I watched, the snake stretched across an open space to another limb and slowly vanished into a knothole, perhaps looking for an early nest of chickadee or titmouse eggs. The balmy weather even coaxed a gleaming yellow cloudless sulfur butterfly from its winter hiding spot. Spring had indeed arrived.

In mid-March, ospreys suddenly reappeared from their southern wintering grounds and reclaimed the previous year's nests as they circled overhead with high-pitched whistles. At Bear Island Wildlife Management Area, both lesser and greater yellowlegs, many of these present in the area all winter, plucked invertebrates from the mud flats while avocets, a winter resident getting ready to leave, swept their long upturned bills through slightly deeper water, where a flock of fifty tundra swans still lingered, along with five white pelicans. Skittish flocks of blue-winged teal mixed with gadwall, shoveler and lesser scaup rose from the water in tightly flying groups, circled and then returned, as they prepared to leave for good. In an isolated wet spot, I found light-green V-shaped sprouts of golden canna lilies just a few inches above the shallow water. In another freshwater wetland, a normally secretive sora rail stepped casually from taller vegetation onto an open raft of frog's-bit and duckweed, pecking at tiny invertebrates among the new shoots of arrowhead. A bald eagle, its white head and massive yellow beak catching the sun, glided into a newly constructed nest where a small movement just above the rim indicated a recently hatched chick. A first few sprigs of toadflax bloomed in the sunny lee of a tractor shed.

In spring, the Bear Island staff lower the water levels in the property's twenty-eight ponds, each in rotation for a few days or a week, constantly exposing new mud flats for migrating shorebirds. In recent years, this management practice has become routine all across the ACE Basin, making the area a key stopover for shorebirds that have lost much of their migrating habitat all along the East Coast flyway. The ability to manipulate water levels to benefit various species throughout the seasons depends on three factors: shallow, diked wetlands; a large tidal range in adjacent rivers; and water control structures known as rice field trunks. The tidal range occurs naturally, but human labor originally created and now maintains the dikes and trunks, a complex system developed centuries ago to grow the famous Carolina Gold rice, the area's premier agricultural crop for 150 years.

On a bright spring morning with the sun just above the horizon, I found the house pond at Bear Island completely drained of its normal eight to sixteen inches of water, exposing forty-two acres of mud flats. The substrate supported a great variety of small crustaceans, marine snails and other mollusks with all manner of annelid worms just below the surface. Yellowlegs, mostly of the lesser variety but with a smattering of taller, more elegant greater yellowlegs, stalked the mud flats singularly and in little groups, picking at this smorgasbord of invertebrates. Stocky, purposeful dowitchers probed deeply with their long bills, pausing occasionally to rise and circle in small flocks, landing again nearby with a flutter of wings.

Dunlins, many already sporting the black belly patch of breeding plumage, wandered among the larger birds, but they, too, seemed restless and subject to short bursts of pointless flight, as if torn between filling up on this bounty or hurrying north to pass on their genes to another generation. Almost overlooked, even smaller shorebirds, collectively known as "peeps," scurried across the mud, picking and probing at this avian banquet. The low sun clearly illuminated the yellow legs of least sandpipers, the key field mark that separates this species from the similar but dark-legged semi-palmated sandpipers. Western sandpipers with their slightly drooping bills seemed strangely absent that day, but the distinctive, more deliberate semi-palmated plovers, like miniature killdeers, dotted the ever-changing avian contingent, all stowing energy for the long flights north to the breeding grounds.

In a sheen of water at the edge of the mud flat, a dozen stately black-necked stilts fed actively, resplendent in formalwear and fashionably slender. In flight, their delicate pink legs extended well beyond their tails as they called, "Yip, yip" to one another. A few stilts stay every year to nest, but like most spring shorebirds in the ACE, the majority just pause for a day or two to feed and rest before flying farther north to breed.

With legs and bills of different lengths and seeking different prey species, migrating shorebirds often segregate themselves by water depth as the water drains from impoundments or as the tide retreats across the salt marsh, but on this morning, with the entire pond surface exposed, the various species mingled together. Among these common migrants, a rarity of sorts lurked, its identification made easier by the exceptionally good light and the proximity of many similar species. Slightly smaller than a lesser yellowlegs with a longer bill that drooped just a bit at the end, stilt sandpipers migrate to and from South America, traveling mostly west of the Mississippi. But that morning, I counted a half dozen stilt sandpipers probing rapidly and dowitcher-like among the other birds and duly noted the greenish legs and rusty cheek patch that distinguish this locally uncommon migrant. In poorer light and without all the common sandpipers for comparison, I might have overlooked these unusual birds.

In the ACE Basin's uplands, March becomes the month for controlled burns to reduce the undergrowth among the southern pines and to prevent a buildup of fuel that might result in a major destructive fire. Controlled burns mimic the natural fires caused by lightning that for centuries maintained the estimated ninety million acres of southern pines that once dominated the Southeast. Today, fire serves as a key management tool to halt plant succession at a point deemed ideal for wildlife and timber production. Uncontrolled by fire, hardwoods would crowd out the pines valued for pulpwood and saw timber. Without regular burning, old fields and wetland edges would grow up in mature brush and trees of lower value to deer, rabbits, turkeys and many other species. Property managers try to burn as much upland acreage as possible every two years or so, first tilling up firebreaks around the designated burn area and then, based on wind conditions, lighting fires around the perimeters of the area and letting them burn toward one another, preventing the establishment of a large, difficult-to-control fire.

With March cool and rainy, Bear Island manager Ross Catterton had fallen behind on his spring burning. Generally, last fall's leaf litter burns well in early March, killing understory saplings and brush before new leaves develop. Some years, however, wet weather delays burning. Toward the end of the month, on a warm, sunny day with little wind, Ross and his staff decided to burn Sampson Island and Hog Island, two Bear Island uplands surrounded by high marsh on one side and impoundments on the other. Here, they needed no fire breaks, depending instead on the wetlands to contain the fire. Sampson Island, just six or eight acres, consisted of mostly mature pines, oaks and sweet gums with an understory of small pine and sweet gum saplings and devil's walking sticks that had grown up during the past couple of years since the last burn. Dripping flaming kerosene from a torch, Ross steered an ATV along the sandy road that skirted the impoundment, leaving behind a weak line of fire that advanced slowly through the rather damp leaf litter with little breeze to push the flames. After the fire had blackened a strip along the road, Ross made several more passes through the open woods, lighting parallel fire lines as he went, until a haze of wispy smoke arose from the entire island. Overhead, tufted titmice and yellow-throated warblers sang, unfazed by the smoke rising through the treetops. But with humidity high, the ground damp from recent rains and the wind light and variable, the burn did not go well. The low flames casually diverged here and there, leaving some spots completely unburned, and never reached high enough or became hot enough to kill the larger understory plants. After doing all they could under the conditions available, the crew moved operations to nearby Hog Island.

In recent years, Hog Island had reverted from planted dove fields to "old field" habitat. Ross plants part of it with native species every few years and allows the rest to grow up in small wax myrtles and other plants that provide cover for many wildlife species and browse for deer. However, a lack of manpower and poor weather conditions had left the twenty-five-acre high spot unburned for seven or eight years. Rows of myrtle bushes, up to fifteen feet tall and of little value to wildlife, interspersed strips of broom sedge. Ross had little trouble igniting the dry stalks of broom sedge, and as the wind picked up and the humidity dropped, the lines of fire snapped and crackled, sending up thick plumes of black smoke. I rode in the ATV through chest-high myrtle bushes, knocking down last year's brittle sesbania stalks and the brown rows of broom sedge. Ross steered with one hand, the other dangling the drip torch over the side, leaving a line of fire in our wake. Large brown grasshoppers flew ahead of us, and a catbird darted out from a row of wax

A controlled burn moves slowly across the forest floor at Bear Island Wildlife Management Area. *Pete Laurie.*

myrtle. But the hot fires, fueled by the dry grass, died quickly when they reached the taller myrtles, leaving them singed but intact, much to Ross's disappointment. He had hoped to scorch these bushes back to the roots so that they could re-sprout and he could maintain them at a height of about four feet with more regular burning.

As the wind shifted to the south, it pushed both fires into the extensive brackish marsh north of the islands. In fits and starts the orange flames leaped from tussock to tussock, not hurting anything, but not really accomplishing much either, according to Ross. With no way to get the ATV into that boggy habitat, Ross and I sat in his pickup and watched the two fires burn while the rest of the crew broke for a late lunch. Ross declared the entire burn about 30 percent successful, about all he could expect this late in the spring.

By mid-March, purple martins had returned to the gourds and martin houses erected around many plantation houses. While welcome and fascinating to watch, martins prey on flies, bees and wasps, eating relatively few mosquitoes despite universally getting credit for doing so. Overnight it seems, another welcome harbinger of spring, the parula warbler, brought its upbeat, buzzy song to the uplands and wooded swamps. Some parulas simply pass through the ACE Basin on their way to nesting grounds located as far north as southern Canada, but many remain to nest in the ACE, often in thick clumps of Spanish moss. A midlevel bird, parulas forage at or below the lower edge of the canopy, making them easier to see and identify than many of spring's treetop warblers. I heard a song sparrow quietly reciting just part of its nesting song over and over one morning as it searched for insects among last year's giant cordgrass stalks. Not far away, a marsh wren, a local nester but not yet ready to nest or to burst into full song, softly practiced its richly jumbled notes as it foraged through cattails just inches above the duckweed surface of a freshwater marsh.

The arrival of spring birds coincides with the gradual departure of winter birds. The tens of thousands of ducks that spent the winter in the ACE Basin gradually disappear, teal often the last to leave. Along beaches, irregular flocks of cormorants, sometimes two hundred or more, fly resolutely north well above the surf. Robins disappear from the swamps, and song sparrows and white throats no longer haunt the thickets. A few winter residents begin to sing before they depart for the northern nesting grounds. Both yellow-rumped warblers and ruby-crowned kinglets commence quiet, complex songs even though they have no intention of nesting anywhere near the South Carolina coast.

In most years, male wild turkeys begin to gobble by the second or third week in March. On still mornings their rapid, descending gobbles roll out of the hardwood bottoms, carrying considerable distances. The single-sex turkey flocks of winter dissolve as the gobblers and hens seek one another out. One March morning, I watched a little flock of four "jakes," young males in their first or second year, dash across a plowed field on Botany Bay Plantation. Their short beards, just three or four inches long, identified them as jakes, although they moved too fast to tell if they lacked the spurs typical of gobblers. Unable to compete with the more experienced older males, jakes sometimes band together in bachelor flocks, for the most part left out of the mating game.

Spring brings sudden splashes of color. The delicate vines of yellow jessamine, the state wildflower, go unnoticed much of the year until they paint the greening shrubs and treetops with strings of little yellow trumpets. Unplowed fields may turn red with sour weed or lemony yellow with wild mustard. In mixed pine-oak forests, redbud, an understory bush or small tree, erupts into a reddish-purple blaze of color. Carolina laurel cherry, horse sugar and Cherokee rose, all early spring bloomers, add a dash of white along the hedgerows and in the open forests. Blue flag, a native iris of wet ditches, joins atamasco lilies along the swamp edges, and coral honeysuckle festoons

Blue flag, a native iris, blooms in early spring in ditches, pond edges and other wet areas.
Pete Laurie.

brushy corners. In a more subtle tone, a spring azure, one of the earliest butterflies, flits close to the ground along mowed dikes and other open areas, showing the pale-blue upper surface of its wings only in flight, the whitish underside visible as it perches with wings folded aloft. On a breezy morning in mid-March, the first palamedes swallowtail of spring floated past me on a woodland trail. Often the most abundant butterflies in wooded areas, palamedes swallowtails (black with yellow striping) appear early in the spring and produce multiple generations throughout the summer. Easy to identify, they fly slowly and directly, visiting a variety of flowers for nectar. Females deposit eggs on red bay, a common understory bush that serves as the larval host plant.

The warm sunny days of spring also activate a less welcome ACE Basin insect: the tiny biting midges known as no-see-ums. Often erroneously referred to as sand gnats, no-see-ums, less than an eighth of an inch long and all but invisible, swarm up from wet spots and disturbed mud onto any exposed skin, where their bites cause at best an irritating itch and at worst considerable swelling and discomfort. They seem to favor early morning and late afternoon, especially near salt marshes and soil with a lot of organic matter, such as manure piles. Both sexes feed on nectar, but the females bite to secure the blood meal needed to produce eggs. Short-lived, they usually peak by early April, sometimes with another population spike in the fall. At times, they can render outdoor work or recreation unbearable.

On the last day of March, I noticed a sudden increase in the small flock of avocets that had wintered at Bear Island. Fifty or sixty of these large shorebirds with the upswept bills worked the shallow water of a partially drawn-down pond. These transients had already developed their spring plumage with an ochre wash on heads and necks. Within another week or two, they would leave for the western plains where they nest. With April just around the corner, wild azaleas had reached full bloom along Bennetts Point Road and in open wooded areas spared from fire for a few years. I stopped to examine the complex pinkish flowers of one of these small shrubs that develop new leaves while they bloom. The sweet fragrance of the blossoms hung in the damp spring air.

A few days into April, I caught a few notes of a familiar bird song I had not heard since the previous summer. I pulled over to the edge of a dirt road that passed through a stand of longleaf pine and got out to scan the treetops. After just a few minutes, I spotted the first summer tanager of the year and a few minutes later a second one, both males in brilliant red plumage. Called "summer redbird" locally to distinguish it from that other "redbird," the cardinal, summer tanagers nest throughout the ACE Basin during May, preferring open pine stands. Later that morning, I recorded another seasonal first, a male orchard oriole in the unusual habitat of giant cordgrass along an impoundment dike, certainly not the horse pastures and

The night-flying chuck-will's-widow, commonly (and incorrectly) called "whippoorwill," often spends daylight hours well camouflaged on the forest floor. *Phillip Jones.*

scattered trees where it usually occurs. Transients and new arrivals, however, often land in atypical habitats after flying all night.

I did not hear the first chuck-will's-widow until just before dawn on April 1. The southern cousin of the whippoorwill and locally given that name, the chuck-will's has quite a different call of four distinct notes repeated more slowly and forcefully than the whippoorwill's rapid three-note call. A bird of the night and especially active and vocal at dusk and just before daybreak, chuck-will's-widows, like all of the clan known as goatsuckers, have short legs and small bills but mouths that can open wide to catch moths and other night-flying insects. They also occasionally catch and swallow small birds such as warblers. During the day they roost on the ground or perch lengthwise on a tree limb. Many people who know of the bird have never seen one. Throughout the spring and summer nesting period, they call repeatedly, often hundreds of times without stopping, at a rate of about twenty-eight times per minute. I once counted a particularly vocal chuck-will's call from the same location 2,116 times without pause. It then flew off one hundred yards or so and called without stopping for another fifteen minutes.

Another spring morning, I cruised slowly along Fields Point Road, which cuts through Chehaw-Combahee Plantation to a public boat ramp on the Combahee River. Open stands of longleaf pine dominated the landscape.

In the sandy soil along this road, longleaf pine, the grandest of the southern pines, seemed to have an advantage over the faster-growing loblolly and slash pines. Below the pines, a rich green ground cover consisting mainly of waist-high scuppernong and pignut hickory sprouts had emerged from the last burning, probably two years earlier. On the edges of the road, small southern red oaks and hickories had survived the regular burning, and a few pignut hickories had reached reproductive maturity and sported green nuts sprouting upward from the ends of last year's twigs. Otherwise, only the longleaf pines had reached maturity in this fire-managed environment.

Many of the longleaf showed new light-green cones. These cones, the largest of the southern yellow pines, grow up to ten inches in length. Cone production usually begins when the tree reaches the age of twenty to thirty years and goes through cycles, with most trees producing just a few cones some years and reaching maximum cone production every five to seven years. The large seeds—each cone holds fifty to sixty—fall to the ground packed with sufficient moisture and nutrients to sprout at once, especially if landing on mineral soil exposed by fire. Since many birds and animals consume longleaf seeds, cyclical cone production helps to keep these seed predators in check so that they can never become abundant enough to consume the entire annual crop, ensuring that a few seeds survive to sprout.

Southern yellow pines lose their horizontal limbs as they grow, creating a habitat consisting of two distinct layers: the dense ground cover and, thirty to forty feet higher, the pine canopy. Open space in between these two distinct zones gives this habitat a park-like appearance. Not surprisingly, the two layers develop quite different faunal communities, with bird life the most visual and vocal. Throughout the canopy, I could hear the distinctive calls of both white-breasted nuthatches and their smaller, chattier brown-headed relatives. The rolling call of red-bellied woodpeckers mixed with the occasional rapid stammer of smaller downy woodpeckers. Where a few of the big pines had died, I caught the black-and-white flash of redheaded woodpeckers as they worked from tree to tree, the red heads of both sexes bright in the patchy sun. The trill of pine warblers mixed with the insistent "pic-a-tuck-a-tuck" of summer tanagers and the plaintive calls of wood peewees. A harsh, hissing cry brought my gaze to the very tip of a longleaf, where a red-tailed hawk proclaimed its territory loudly before flying off, perhaps to hunt cotton rats or other small mammals or perhaps to feed nestlings.

Understory birds, while also quite vocal, mostly remained out of sight. The unmistakably concise calls of bobwhite quail rang out every few minutes, although I saw only two. They appeared suddenly in the road and

Black root, common in longleaf pines and other areas with sandy soil, blooms in May and June. *Pete Laurie.*

ran ahead of my pickup for one hundred yards or more. Finally turning with a panicked look, they leapt into the air, curved around a solitary post oak and vanished. Unseen towhees called their own name from the thick underbrush, and the familiar "chip" of cardinals came from all sides, as did the ringing songs of Carolina wrens. I tried to tune out these familiar bird sounds as I listened for what Roger Tory Peterson calls the "clear liquid whistle" of the most secretive bird of the pine savannahs, Bachman's sparrow, sometimes called simply the "pine woods sparrow." Audubon named this bird for his friend John Bachman, who discovered it near Charleston in 1832.

Silent and rarely seen during much of the year, male Bachman's sparrows sing during only the spring and early summer nesting season. I thought I heard a couple singing in the distance as I drove along slowly, stopping often, but I certainly did not expect to see one. But then a small bird flew into a low dead sweet gum, threw back its head until its bill pointed straight up and began to whistle a dreamy tune followed by a jumble of short notes. Just one hundred feet off the road, it showed a plain buffy breast, which, with the song, habitat and behavior, identified it at once as the usually secretive Bachman's sparrow. It obligingly sat in the same spot, singing every fifteen seconds or so, for a least five minutes.

In spring, Bachman's sparrow and the other seed eaters switch their diet to mostly insects and insect larvae, which they also feed to their young nestlings, which cannot digest hard seeds. The treetop habitat in the pinewoods no doubt develops an entirely different insect community than does the ground cover just twenty or thirty feet below. As a result, canopy birds and understory birds in the same habitat and just a few yards apart probably feed on entirely different insects. I also watched several species of flycatchers preying on insects flying through the open strata between the two layers of green. Wood peewees—along with smaller Acadian flycatchers and the larger, brash great-crested flycatchers—hunted from lookouts on dead limbs just below the canopy or from the tips of the ground plants. At one point, a very active family of great-crested flycatchers chased one another with much swooping, abrupt changes of course and enthusiastic cries of "wheep" as recently fledged young hassled their parents for food—all part of the youngsters' learning to find their own food and fend for themselves.

Abruptly, the sandy road dipped down five or six feet, and instantly the habitat changed from open pine savannah to low, wooded swamp of sweet gum, red maple and live oak festooned with resurrection fern and Spanish moss. Here, the open layer between ground and canopy vanished as standing water choked with duckweed and emergent vegetation climbed upward into a tangle of honeysuckle, poison ivy and Virginia creeper vines into a continuous green maze that climbed into the treetops. A startled green heron sprang from a patch of lizard tail to quickly vanish into the tangle with a surprised squawk. A parula warbler repeated its sneezy little song, and a yellow-throated warbler's clear notes, mixed with the warble of a white-eyed vireo, filled the heavy damp air. Somewhere in the green tangle, a bullfrog called "jug-of-rum," and a few southern chorus frogs trilled in response. As in much of the ACE Basin, water always remains close at hand, and just a few feet of elevation change allowed for a complete metamorphosis in both plants and animals. This little slough no doubt drained into the nearby Combahee River and after heavy rain probably held much more water, perhaps never completely drying except during prolonged drought.

After about fifty yards, the road just as abruptly rose back to the sandy open pine-oak forest. Here, the sparse undergrowth suggested a more recent burn, probably just a few months earlier. At one open spot that probably had held water a few weeks previously, several clumps of carnivorous hooded pitcher plant had grown up in tight phalanxes, their odor attracting several flies. The high water table and hardpan just below the surface favored pitcher plants and another common plant of this habitat, toothache grass.

From the thick foliage of a young live oak, a male rufous-sided towhee sang, "Drink your teeeeea" as a female cowbird watched alertly, probably searching for the towhee's likely nearby nest. Cowbirds, much less common in South Carolina just fifty years ago, now have greatly increased in population. Building no nest of her own, the female cowbird lays her eggs in the nests of other birds, usually smaller species. The larger cowbird chick often hatches first and then pushes the other chicks from the nest, leaving the parent birds to rear this unwanted foster child. Most birds have such an attachment to their nestlings that they seem not to notice as they work tirelessly to raise this very large chick of a different species. In the ACE Basin, cowbirds often target towhees, along with painted buntings, indigo buntings, blue grosbeaks and chipping sparrows. Considering that cowbirds generally lay one egg per nest and may lay ten to twelve eggs per nesting season, these parasitic birds have a considerable negative impact on small birds. Years ago, cowbirds, denizens of open fields and forest edges, did not threaten woodland nesting birds. Today, however, cowbirds enjoy greater access to wooded areas as highways and power line right of ways have carved up large forested tracts, providing many entry points for cowbirds. The ACE Basin's extensive unbroken woodlands, with few roads or power lines, limit the parasitic cowbird populations and offer a haven for many nesting songbirds.

The ACE Basin's earliest rice planters attempted an "inland" system, using rainfall as a source of water to flood the growing rice. After clearing wooded swamps and the streams that connected them to the area's three rivers, they constructed dikes to divide the waterway into fields, the uppermost area serving as a reserve to hold rainwater. With sufficient rainfall, water from the reserve could flood the lower fields as needed while excess water could

Fiddleheads, the developing leaves of ferns, erupt across the spring uplands. *Pete Laurie.*

drain out the low end of the system into the river. The inland rice-growing system worked well with the right amount of rainfall. However, years of drought left rice planters with insufficient water to flood the growing rice crop. Excessive rainfall pushed water over the reserve's dike and washed out the rice crop in the lower fields. After about forty years, planters abandoned this unpredictable system in favor of a tidally driven system, using the predictable and consistent daily rise and fall of the tides to flood and drain the rice fields.

Remnants of these ancient inland rice culture systems still exist throughout the ACE Basin, some of them still more or less functional, and provide habitat for waterfowl, wading birds, shore birds and many other species. Donnelley Wildlife Management Area contains an excellent example of the inland rice-growing system. I stopped by the old reserve that supplied water to this system on a late spring morning to watch the bird activity. From the original system's uppermost dike, I could see dozens of white wading birds among the green foliage of small cypress trees growing in the shallow water. Through binoculars I could identify wood storks, along with great and snowy egrets, all sitting or standing on flimsy stick nests. This rookery, one of dozens in the ACE Basin, provides ideal nesting conditions for these wading birds, which seek trees or bushes growing above standing water to discourage raccoons and other nest predators. Raccoons swim quite well, of course, but avoid wetlands populated by alligators, so they mostly leave these nesting birds alone. For their part, the gators eagerly snatch up any chicks that fall from their nests, but these have little chance of survival anyway. So the gators, without intending to, greatly increase the nesting success of storks, egrets, herons, anhingas and other colonial nesters.

On a muggy, overcast morning, I joined DNR biologist Kristin Brunk on her weekly monitoring of this wood stork rookery. With spring well advanced, the woods and wetlands, although still a shade lighter than the mature shade of summer, had turned a lush green. We walked to the middle of a dike built centuries ago to hold reserve water for the area's rice field complex. Kristin set up a spotting scope and began to scan the wood stork nests at the far end of the reserve, comparing what she saw with previously noted stork nests that she had indicated in red pencil on photographs taken earlier. We could see only a few actual nests, just flimsy platforms of a few sticks, but each such active nest held one or both adult storks, long white forms against the green of the little cypress trees that held the nests.

Wood storks generally produce four or five eggs, and once the female deposits the first egg in the nest, both birds develop such an attachment to that spot that one of the pair remains at the nest at all times. Through the scope, we could see ten or twelve nests, each of which held one or two of the motionless birds. At some nests, the pair stood side by side. At others, one bird stood while the other crouched on the nest, perhaps incubating eggs, a chore shared by both parents. As befitting this always solemn, dignified-looking bird, the nesting storks stood stoically, showing no aggression toward nesting neighbors, even when sharing the same branch just a few feet apart. Kristin noted five new nests since last week, explaining that the birds, at least in this season, had not all started nesting at the same time. Panning the scope across the reserve, we could see a few other species nesting here as well, including great egrets and anhingas.

Kristin then shouldered the tripod and we continued across the dike into the mixed hardwood forest, where we followed a wide firebreak that circled around to the upper end of the reserve. The moist woods rang with the songs of spring. Parula and yellow-throated warblers, joined by summer tanagers, proclaimed their territories with constant, repetitious melodies. Among all that sound I heard the first wood peewee of spring calling its name and, a few minutes later, the clear, liquid song of a recently arrived wood thrush, perhaps just passing through since wood thrushes seldom nest in the ACE Basin. Off in the distance, a turkey gobbled. We continued along the firebreak as it skirted the edge of the reserve until we reached another dike, this one narrow and little used. From the dike's tall grass ahead of us a seven-foot gator got up, walked to the edge of the dike and splashed through the emergent vegetation into the shallow water.

Crossing the dike, we continued along the wooded edge of the wetland until a small opening offered a view of more stork nests at this upper end of the reserve. Kristin noted several more new nests as we moved to a couple more openings. At one spot, we could see several stork nests in a small spreading loblolly pine. Again, the rookery remained quiet and sedate with the patient storks standing or sitting on their little stick platforms. In rookeries with few nesting sites and lots of birds, storks can get quite aggressive as they compete for space, Kristin said, but at this rookery, where good nesting sites abound, the birds nested in peace with their neighbors. By our last stop, we had recorded ten new nests, bringing the total for the rookery to forty, with as many as one hundred eventually expected.

Stork eggs hatch in about twenty-eight days, the chicks staying in the nest for about eight weeks before they fledge. When the chicks reach about four weeks of age, Kristin and her supervisor, Christy Hand, planned to canoe out to the nest trees and band as many chicks as

The ACE Basin's most common rattlesnake, the canebreak or timber rattler, prefers wooded areas. *Phillip Jones.*

possible to learn more about wood stork movements throughout the year. Not all chicks survive to fledge; experts consider an average of two per nest a successful nesting season. Previous studies suggest that the adults return each spring to the same rookeries, perhaps even the same tree or nest platform. Chicks, which will not reach maturity until the age of four or five, exhibit no affinity to their natal rookery, eventually dispersing to other, distant habitats.

Areas with ideal conditions for rookeries do not always provide good foraging habitat, so all these nesting birds must travel considerable distances to feed—wood storks go as much as twenty miles—returning with partially digested food that they regurgitate to feed the nestlings. All these comings and goings fill the air with activity, quite in contrast to the birds sitting on eggs or protecting just hatched chicks. Wood storks, just recently downgraded from endangered to threatened, began nesting in South Carolina just thirty years or so ago after losing wetland habitat in Florida. Once just a casual late summer visitor to the South Carolina coast, wood storks now nest in a number of coastal rookeries, with 2,500 nests counted in South Carolina in 2014, many of those in the ACE Basin. Without the basin's extensive, well-maintained wetlands, the wood stork population, with nowhere else to go, might have suffered even greater decline.

In Florida, wood storks establish rookeries over flowing water, but the still water of the old rice plantation reserves they favor here can allow mats of frog's-bit, pennywort and swamp loosestrife to develop under the rookery. This vegetation creates a land bridge for raccoons and possums to reach the nests without encountering alligators. Herbicides can control this vegetation, but spraying during the nesting season disrupts the birds and might cause them to abandon the rookery. However, offseason treatment reduces the growth of these vegetative mats, and wood storks in recent years have enjoyed excellent nesting success.

A more recent addition to the bird life of these old rice field reserves, the black-bellied whistling duck first arrived in the ACE Basin in 1993 and now nests throughout the area. A native of the coast from Texas south to Argentina, these long-legged, long-necked and quite colorful waterfowl expanded their range eastward and now have gained resident status in the ACE. After twenty years, these odd-looking ducks with their pink bills paddling sedately among the white blooms of the lily pads have become part of the ACE Basin experience. Whistling ducks occasionally nest in holes in trees, as well as in wood duck boxes, but they do not appear to compete with wood ducks, which nest earlier in the year.

Another locally nesting duck, the mottled duck—not quite so new and not arriving under its own power—prefers the ACE Basin's extensive grassy impoundments over wooded swamps or the rice culture reserves. In the 1970s and 1980s, DNR biologists brought in the nonmigratory mottled ducks from Louisiana with the idea that they would nest in the state and provide additional waterfowl hunting opportunities. The state's mottled duck population has since slowly grown to an estimated twenty-two thousand birds, many of which live in the ACE Basin. Very similar in appearance to black ducks, mottled ducks generally associate in pairs, seldom large flocks. Black ducks, some years quite common in the ACE Basin during the late fall and winter, migrate north to breed, leaving mottled ducks as the only "black duck" in South Carolina during the summer.

In a study begun in 2008, biologists, using an airboat to cruise through the shallow marshes at night, captured mottled ducks with dip nets. They banded and released 3,400 birds, fitted 45 hens with backpack transmitters and implanted transmitters into an additional 145 birds. Tracking data indicate that the majority of the locally captured birds spent their entire lives within the ACE Basin, with 95 percent preferring impounded wetlands to natural tidal marsh. They also showed a preference for brackish marshes over freshwater wetlands or agricultural fields. A few banded birds, almost all adult males, roamed to inland South Carolina, Georgia or North Carolina, but in general, mottled ducks have small home ranges. Another study located 53 mottled duck nests, which held an average clutch of eight eggs per nest. Nesting hens prefer the edges of dikes and islands of vegetation in impoundments. Hens with broods stayed in water up to six inches deep with a home range of 330 acres. Although the introduction of mottled ducks has added slightly to the state's duck population, the effort has not displaced any native waterfowl and apparently caused no harm,

A bird that historically caused great harm, the bob-o-link, now passes quickly through the ACE Basin each spring drawing little notice. Members of the blackbird family, bob-o-links winter in South America and nest in meadows and hayfields from West Virginia to as far north as Canada. One April morning, I heard the constant gurgling chatter of a small flock hidden in a weedy field at Bear Island WMA. Suddenly, about thirty birds flew up into view, the males resplendent in their black-and-white spring plumage while the yellowish tinge of the females caught the sunlight as they circled once and settled back down. Male bob-o-links have reversed the normal color pattern of many birds, usually dark above and light below. Instead, these unique birds sport white patches on their upper surface with a cream-colored nape while the underside remains solid black. The distinctive coloration makes this bird one of the easiest to identify of any North American species. The flashing pattern of the males, the endless bubbling calls of the flock and their restless enthusiasm brighten any spring day.

However, for 150 years, this little bird, which often migrates in flocks of one thousand or more, drew the wrath of rice planters along the tidal rivers. Bob-o-links usually arrived just after the spring planting. The green rice sprouts pinpointed the location of each planted grain, and bob-o-links went down every row, pulling up the sprouts and devouring the carefully planted seeds as they went, wiping out entire fields. The planters fired guns and slaves patrolled the dikes banging on pots and pans in futile attempts to keep the hungry "rice birds" moving. In the fall, these same birds returned just at harvest time, often destroying a great deal of the rice crop. However, in fall, the males had molted into a plumage almost identical to the brown, streaky females. The rice planters, not comprehending such a profound change in appearance, considered the fall birds a different species. Today, with the rice culture just a memory, few people still call them "rice birds," and without the thousands of acres of rice to feed them, bob-o-links do not tarry long in the ACE Basin during either spring or fall.

As spring, with all its sights and sounds, progresses across the uplands, another type of equally feverish activity takes place silently below the ebb and flow of the ACE Basin's ninety thousand acres of tidal marsh. Here, the meandering creeks provide a pathway for larval fish, shrimp and crabs spawned offshore to seek the protected, nutrient-rich marsh. Up to 95 percent of marsh creek fauna consists of larvae or juvenile animals. On each incoming tide, these minute animals rise to the surface, where the current runs strongest, and then drop to the bottom on the outgoing tide, netting an inland movement on each tide. The youngest animals seek the headwaters of the smallest creeks and then gradually work their way downstream as they grow and mature, feasting on a rich soup of decaying marsh vegetation (detritus), plankton and other organic matter. To avoid competition for food, the larvae of various species stagger their creek invasions with the seasons. Salinities in creeks vary from seawater strength to freshwater levels depending on the stage of the tide and the amount of rainfall. The variation requires that all these animals have a tolerance for widely ranging and sometimes quickly changing salinities. By spring, the winter population of larval flounder, pinfish, mullet and spot have long since left the nursery areas, replaced by the larvae of spotted seatrout and brown shrimp, which by summer will give way to the larvae of white shrimp and blue crabs. Marine animals with long spawning seasons, such as spotted seatrout, produce several waves of creek larvae throughout the year.

Larger predators, such as adult red drum, flounder and seatrout, avoid the shallow, muddy waters of the small creeks, where temperatures during the summer can soar with a corresponding drop in dissolved oxygen. With the falling tide, these predators congregate at the mouths of these small creeks to snatch up juvenile animals pushed into deeper water as the creeks run dry. On the rising tide, as it spills out of the creeks and washes in a shallow sheen across the grassy marsh surface, creek inhabitants can escape the larger aquatic predators, but at the same time, they expose themselves to avian predators of several species.

That all these organisms can thrive and develop in the marsh and feed the many aquatic and avian predators, plus provide the bulk of local seafood, including shrimp, crabs, oysters and a variety of fishes, attests to the tremendous productivity of the salt marsh. Sadly, this key habitat went unappreciated and often destroyed for centuries due simply to a lack of understanding of the salt marsh's unusual food web. In most grassy habitats, herbivores, often large and conspicuous, consume the vegetative growth in an obvious food chain. But the soft substrate of the salt marsh excludes large plant eaters, and the huge expanses of spartina go unconsumed throughout the growing season. In the fall, the grasses die back, the brittle stalks broken down by wind and currents. Finally, bacteria consume the bits of grass into the rich soup of detritus that forms the basis of the unusual salt marsh food chain.

Mats of floating spartina from the previous year often get pushed by wind and tides up against the causeway to the beach at Botany Bay WMA. The causeway on this former private plantation, willed to the state in 2008 and now managed by the DNR, offers the unique opportunity to walk through a salt marsh without getting your feet wet. On a spring morning, I set out across this causeway, which begins at a small wooden bridge that spans a deep, narrow creek threading its way through the high marsh that stretches unbroken into the distance, east and west. Low tide had exposed a scattering of small oysters, and from the mud, snapping shrimp popped like little firecrackers. An otter, unaware of my presence, swam smoothly under the bridge and up the narrow stream still trickling seaward. Where the water deepened, the otter dove beneath the surface and vanished without a ripple. Otters serve as one of the top marsh predators, consuming snails, shrimp, crabs, terrapins and a variety of fish species. Powerful swimmers, capable of running down and catching almost any fish, otters also often travel extensively over land. Like other mammals, they feed in the salt marsh, coming and going with the tide, but do not actually live in the marsh. During the late winter breeding season, they den on high ground, keeping their newborn kits warm and dry above the tide.

As I continued along the causeway, fiddler crabs and mud crabs, alert to the movement of approaching predators, stood sentinel at their mud burrows. Hundreds of periwinkles, the common marsh snail, inched their way up the grass stalks, grazing on algae and other organic material that coated the stunted plants, so different from the tall spartina stalks that grow along the well-flushed banks of the larger creeks in the lower salt marsh. A dozen whimbrels in a loose flock towered over the sparse grass stalks as they probed for the abundant fiddlers, extracting them from their holes and gulping them down. These large shorebirds, abundant in spring and fall, fly to the Arctic to nest and then immediately return toward their South American wintering grounds, on some years passing back through the ACE Basin as early as July.

The Botany Bay causeway eventually reaches a marsh hummock, one of 3,500 of these little islands that dot the state's extensive salt marshes. As development continues to alter much of the mainland coast, these high spots—some many acres, others better measured in square feet—have increasingly become critical habitat to nesting and migrant birds, such as painted buntings. The Botany Bay hummock supports red cedar, palmetto and live oak, all species that can tolerate some salt. Along the island's sandy fringe, reached by only the very highest of tides, stunted sea ox-eye grows along with isolated patches of salicornia, also called salt pickle. Another short stretch of causeway brought me to the ribbon of high ground behind the beach. This narrow strip, the remains of a maritime forest, supported a few live oaks and large palmettos, a coastal tree capable of withstanding tropical storm–force winds. In a few more steps, I reached the beach, whose sands encroach into the remains of the forest.

Although suffering from severe erosion in recent years, the beach at Botany Bay still provides habitat for the only two beach nesting shorebird species of the ACE Basin: the American oystercatcher and Wilson's plover. In mid-April, DNR biologist Janet Thibault invited me to join her as she monitored the nesting progress of these two locally threatened species. Both oystercatchers and Wilson's plovers have lost much of their nesting habitat to beachfront development, human disturbance and erosion during the past decades, leaving them with fewer and fewer suitable places to nest. At a little past seven o'clock in the morning, with the tide dead low, we walked briskly south along the shell-strewn sand just below the high tide mark. At the crest of the low-profile beach, a line of orange string, supported every fifty feet or so by slender wooden posts with "Do Not Enter" signs, marked the potential nesting habitat for these birds. We soon reached Frampton Inlet, a narrow, constantly shifting slough that drains the hundreds of acres of salt marsh behind the beach. Still flowing into the ocean, the clear water almost topped our knee boots. We waded quickly across to Interlude Beach.

Here, a second line of orange string greeted us. We followed the string several hundred yards until it wound around the beach crest to another inlet, the limit of the Botany Bay Plantation beach. We ducked under the string and began searching for the shallow scrapes that serve as nests for both species. A nervous oystercatcher kept its distance, eying us cautiously with a quiet, nervous piping. Janet, consulting her field notes from three days earlier, soon located the first scrape, then a second about twenty feet away and finally a third about the same distance beyond that. This third scrape held the season's first actual nesting sign: a single grayish-brown egg with dark splotches, superbly camouflaged among the broken bits of shell that littered the sand. Delighted with this find, Janet placed a small blue marker about ten feet from the scrape and recorded the position in her notebook.

Not wanting to disturb the bird, we moved quickly away and began searching for new scrapes and checking the scrapes Janet had located earlier.

The males of both of these species usually construct the scrapes by pushing their bellies into the sand and kicking their feet out behind, creating a shallow depression that would often go undetected except for the bird tracks in the surrounding sand. The much smaller plovers generate scrapes hardly larger than a saucer, often adjacent to one or more small sticks or other debris to protect it from blowing sand and usually very difficult to locate. As a rule, each male creates three scrapes, generally in a straight line. The female then selects one scrape for egg laying. Territorial, the mated pairs of each species keep a distance of many yards between their sets of scrapes. The nesting area occupied the highest strip of the beach but still rested just a couple of feet above the normal high tide mark, and therefore, big tides regularly overwashed it. We carefully crisscrossed this fenced-off area, finding a few more scrapes of both species but no more eggs. After an hour and a half, we had worked our way back to Frampton Inlet, just in time to get back across, as the now rising tide had already begun to surge back toward the marsh, the current now stronger and forcing us to pick and choose our course to avoid deep channels until we finally regained the other side.

We now could proceed at a more leisurely pace as we searched this roped-off nesting area, eventually finding scrapes Janet had recorded earlier, along with a few new ones. With most of the birds off feeding at low tide, we saw only a few adult oystercatchers or plovers. We did see otter tracks throughout the nesting area, although the raccoons probably do the most damage, consuming any eggs they can locate. At one point, a female Wilson's plover went into its broken wing act, shuffling along the sand with one wing dragging as if injured, a standard ploy meant to draw a predator away from a nest. Of the two birds, only the plover utilizes the wing dragging behavior, and while it suggested the presence of eggs, we never could find a scrape in the area, let alone one with eggs. We withdrew about a hundred yards and sat quietly on an old palmetto log on the back edge of the beach to watch the bird through binoculars. However, it simply stood at a little high spot, showing no interest in returning to a nest, as we enjoyed the light breeze off the ocean and listened to marsh wrens in the adjacent marsh sing their cheerful, jumbled little songs. We finally gave up and moved on with our search, locating a few additional scrapes but never any more eggs. The sun had climbed well into the sky, and the temperature had risen a good bit by the time we finished the nest monitoring for that day. The DNR had additional trips planned every three days for the next couple of months. Janet hoped that this first ever structured nest monitoring on Botany Bay beach would provide information on the nesting success and failure of these two species.

A week later, I checked this same beach and found three oystercatcher nests with a total of seven eggs and the area's first Wilson plover nest of the year, which contained two eggs, equally well camouflaged but smaller than the oystercatchers' eggs. Recent rain and a strong breeze had obliterated any bird tracks, making scrapes even more of a challenge to locate. Just a few days before a new moon, the higher tide made the inlet more difficult to cross, and my knee boots filled with water as I crossed over to Interlude Beach and back. The unprotected eggs sitting on the low-profile beach require twenty-eight days to hatch for the oystercatcher and twenty-five for the plover, so these vulnerable nests must survive the potential overwash of several new moon and full moon tides. Should the tides destroy the nests, as often happens here, both species will attempt to nest again.

West of the little settlement of Ritter, where the upper reaches of the Ashepoo and Combahee Rivers flow just a few miles apart, South Carolina Highway 41 crosses the Ashepoo, here only a few yards wide. Next to the bridge, fishermen have carved out a little parking spot on the road's shoulder, barely enough room for a couple of vehicles to pull off the pavement. Miles from the ocean, the river still ran languidly upstream on a rising tide, and the spring air rang with the forceful "chee, chee, chee" of prothonotary warblers. A bright-yellow male paused on a broken piling from a previous bridge and then raced off after another male as they jockeyed for nesting territory. With a quick "smack" an unseen fish snatched a water scavenger beetle from the dark, swirling water. Somewhere above in the canopy of cypress, tupelo and red maple came the staccato call of a yellow-billed cuckoo.

Continuing a few miles to the southeast, I turned down White Hall Road and after a few miles stopped in at a rather primitive boat landing on Cuckold's Creek, a tributary of the Combahee River. Just across the creek, thick grasses, mostly cattails, replaced the wooded habitat of the upper Ashepoo. A pair of red-bellied woodpeckers worked the few dead cypress trees that rose among the grass. Two Saturday morning bank fishermen, supplied with a variety of baits including shrimp and crickets, had enjoyed some luck. A five-gallon plastic bucket held two warmouth, a small white catfish and an even smaller yellow bullhead—all considered freshwater species, although white catfish do stray into brackish water and warmouth can tolerate some salinity, up to four parts per thousand. The numerous fiddler crabs around the edges of the concrete landing suggested a brackish environment, but fiddlers, too, do quite well in a wide range of salinities. With shrimp as bait for saltwater

Buttonbush, a shrub or small tree, grows along the edges of wetlands throughout the ACE Basin, blooming in early summer. *Pete Laurie.*

fishes and crickets to entice freshwater species, these obviously experienced anglers understood the shifting dynamics of fish populations in many ACE Basin streams and had come prepared. To successfully inhabit these sections of the three rivers where salinity can change rapidly, animals must have a high tolerance for such sudden and sometimes drastic shifts. Fish can simply move up or down stream when heavy rainfall drops salinity or exceptionally high tides push brackish water farther inland. The less mobile crabs have fewer options, retreating to the more stable environment of their burrows when conditions become stressful.

In late spring along the upper reaches of the basin's three rivers, redbreast sunfish begin to spawn and to attract the considerable attention of freshwater fishermen. Seldom reaching more than half a pound but fun to play on light tackle and excellent table fare, these colorful fish vary in numbers in any given year based on environmental conditions. On a sunny late April day, I met DNR biologist Chris Thomason at a remote boat ramp about forty river miles up the Edisto to check on the redbreast population. We launched Thomason's sixteen-foot aluminum shock boat into the Edisto's slowly swirling waters, which stood just at flood stage. Out of its banks and still rising after recent rains, the river had surged into the hardwoods that lined the main channel, greatly expanding its width. This boded well for redbreast and, indeed, for all the river's inhabitants, Thomason said, but we probably would not have much luck shocking fish. For the past few springs, Thomason has used the shock boat, which stuns fish but does not kill them, to collect redbreast adults that he then takes to a hatchery in Barnwell for spawning. The fingerlings produced at the hatchery he can chemically mark for identification and then release into the river. The following year, he collects adult redbreast from the stocking area. In a normal year, the stocked fish, easily identified from the chemical mark on their ear bones, make up about 10 percent of the population, significant enough, he said, to justify the effort.

We eased slowly up the river, lined with black willows, light green in their spring foliage and with dangling strings of flowers. Behind the willows stood tall cypress and shortleaf pine, along with many oaks and other hardwoods. Above the sound of the idling outboard engine, we could hear the songs and calls of white-eyed vireos, yellow-throated warblers and summer tanagers. A large spiny soft-shelled turtle had pulled itself onto a slanted log to bask at the edge of the channel. The tan, flattened shell and pointed snout identified it at once even from a distance. The high water had covered all sandbars and other channel structures and surrounded some of the fishing cabins and weekend retreats along the river's east side. At flood stage, the broad flood plain becomes accessible to redbreast and other fishes that can move in to prey on crayfish, insects, small mollusks and other invertebrates. The flood plain, according to Thomason, provides the energy for the entire river system. In drought years, when the river never rises out of the channel, redbreast and all other species suffer. This winter and early spring, Thomason noted with satisfaction, the water had risen into the surrounding forest three times, providing redbreast with plenty of food and leaving them in good shape for the upcoming spawning season.

Along a steep limestone cliff, we cranked up the generator and dropped the electrodes into the dark water. With Thomason running the boat, I stood on the raised deck at the bow, dip net at the ready. As we drifted sideways downstream, Thomason held the bow close to the overhanging branches of cypress and willow. A couple of longnose gar rolled at the surface, and I netted a large carp just to practice with the net but saw no redbreast. We tried several other spots, even venturing a short ways into the flood plain at one point without much action. I did net a mudfish and then an American shad, which Thomason examined briefly and determined a male that had already spawned. We never did catch a redbreast, but Thomason said the river needed to drop about five feet before he expected to have much luck. Once the water level drops later in the spring, redbreast move back into the channel, where they spawn on sandy shallow bottoms. As we headed back to the landing, enjoying the spring weather, Thomason told how flathead catfish—a voracious, nonnative predator somehow introduced into the Edisto about twenty years ago—had decimated the redbreast population. With the flathead population now stabilized, the redbreast's had rebounded, although several years of drought had kept the population below normal until just recently. Based on what he had seen that morning, Thomason predicted another good year for redbreast, the targeted species for up to 70 percent of freshwater fishermen in ACE Basin streams.

The winter and early spring rains would keep the Edisto at flood stage for a while longer, but much of the ACE Basin uplands had mostly dried out by late April. One morning at Donnelley WMA, I drove past technicians on big tractors planting the carefully prepared fields in corn, sesame and other grains for next fall's dove shoot. In the open pine stands, new green grasses and ferns had sprouted from the bare forest floor, still black from the controlled burns of a few weeks ago. At the end of a short causeway, I surprised an immature Cooper's hawk plucking a common gallinule it had just killed. The hawk tried to fly off with its prey but, finding it too heavy to lift, dropped the carcass and flew up into a small tree. Then, with a few flaps of its short, rounded wings, it glided off across the adjacent wetland. I walked over to the unfortunate gallinule, its long, greenish toes still twitching slightly. The hawk had consumed the bird's brain and had succeeded in plucking the feathers from the head and neck. I moved on quickly, hoping the hawk would return to finish its meal.

By May, the days had grown hot and languid with plenty of mosquitoes and yellow-billed cuckoos calling from dense foliage on muggy, overcast afternoons. I watched a male house finch feed a fledgling as it crouched fluttering along the edge of a sunflower field. Not far away, a female cardinal tended to several twittering youngsters, their tails still short and their heavy bills yet to turn red. Under overhanging branches of a large live oak festooned with Spanish moss, a lone wood stork waded slowly through an isolated slough still holding several inches of water. It carefully dangled first one pink foot and then the other in the shallow water, hoping to cause some reaction from any aquatic organism it could then snap up with its heavy gray beak. Occasionally, it flared out one of its long wings as if to shade its eyes to better see through the soupy water as it moved with the unhurried pace of the upcoming summer.

SUMMER

Spring slips smoothly into summer in the ACE Basin. Long days, combined with high temperatures and humidity, provide ideal conditions for plant growth and for the activities of exothermic (coldblooded) reptiles, amphibians, insects and many other invertebrates. Aquatic organisms, both fishes and invertebrates, also thrive as summer weather warms the ACE Basin's extensive and varied aquatic habitats. Meanwhile, birds continue nesting during early summer. While the males become showy and vocal as they proclaim their territories, the females turn quiet and secretive, sitting on eggs or feeding nestlings. Bird watchers expect no surprises, no rare birds at this season as populations and movements become stable and predictable. Signs of nesting abound, but actually finding the usually well-concealed nests of any species requires some effort.

I joined Beau Bauer early on a June morning as he prowled Nemours Plantation's ten thousand acres searching for nesting wild turkeys. Midway through his second season of tracking radio-tagged hen turkeys, Bauer had learned a good bit about their habits but still had more questions than answers. As a Nemours Wildlife Foundation wildlife biologist, Bauer sought to document the habitat preferences for turkey nesting and brood rearing. Researchers have conducted similar studies at various parts of the wild turkey's extensive North American range but never before in the ACE Basin.

Placing a radio receiver on the floor of his pickup and attaching it by cable to an antenna extending above the cab, he described how in late winter, when the hens remained in flocks, he had captured eighteen last year and twelve this year using a rocket net set over an open area baited with corn. On each bird he had fitted a small transmitter held in place by inserting the wings through a harness that secured the device without disrupting the bird's normal range of motion. Once the breeding season commenced, the radio-tagged hens dispersed to nest. Bauer wanted to know where.

Blooming in early summer, golden canna lilies develop asymmetrical three-petal flowers on tall stalks. *Pete Laurie.*

He had already lost a few tagged birds to predators—bobcats and great-horned owls the most likely culprits, he said. Since each transmitter produced a different signal, he could locate any individual bird by simply switching frequencies on the receiver. We picked up the first bird when the receiver started to beep just a quarter mile from the office. He knew this bird had nested once but had abandoned that nest and now stayed several hundred yards to the west. Hens that abandon a first nest often try again, he said, and he hoped to locate a second nest for this bird.

He stopped and got out to plug the portable receiver into a handheld directional antenna. The steady beep of the receiver soon located the bird in a stand of young longleaf pine. The signal's strength suggested a distance of not much over one hundred yards but with some movement, indicating a foraging hen, not one incubating eggs. He made an entry into his field notebook and, with no need to pursue this bird for the moment, offered to show me the bird's abandoned nest.

Just fifty feet off a well-used plantation road, the hen had placed her first nest at the base of a loblolly pine in a regularly burned area of waist-high undergrowth. Bauer had often seen this pattern of nest site election: near a road or firebreak for easy access and close to a field or other open area that would produce plenty of insects to feed the poults as soon as they left the nest. He thought the spring planting noise of tractors in the field just across the road had disturbed the hen and caused her to abandon the nest.

We then crossed U.S. Highway 17 onto still more Nemours property, where Bauer had tracked an especially elusive bird that might have a nest, but he had never confirmed it.

"This is a tricky hen," he said, shaking his head as the receiver beeped. "I try not to take an anthropomorphic approach to these birds, but they all have different personalities." After slowly bouncing along an overgrown road through oak-pine habitat and across a couple of small, open fields, we finally had a strong enough signal to get out and track the bird on foot. We circled around a low area of dwarf palmetto—not good nesting habitat, Bauer said—and proceeded along a grassy dike. At the border with the Combahee Unit of the Hollings National Wildlife Refuge, a narrow, weedy canal blocked our progress. Part of an old rice field complex, it appeared too deep to wade without getting completely soaked, so we left that hen without learning whether or not she had a nest. Once again, this "tricky" bird had eluded him.

Throughout the morning, Bauer kept up a running commentary on what he had learned so far of the nesting habits of this popular game bird. With the advent of the breeding season, hens disperse as much as five miles from their wintering flocks. After mating, they select a nest site and scrape out a slight depression, often lining it with pine straw. They then lay one egg a day until they have a completed clutch of eight to thirteen eggs. As the clutch increases, they spend more and more of each day sitting on the eggs but may forage up to half a mile away, leaving the nest unprotected. Incubation, which begins in earnest when the hen completes her clutch, lasts an average of twenty-six days. The eggs usually all hatch within twenty-four hours, and the poults leave the nest within a day or two, although the hen may brood them the first couple of nights to keep them warm.

We stopped at one successfully completed nest so Bauer could show me what he considered an ideal placement. From the road, we walked in through second-growth hardwoods to the nest, still littered with broken eggshells. This hen had chosen the base of a post oak with a light understory of switch cane, giving her some cover but allowing the sitting bird to see an approaching raccoon, fox or bobcat. A firebreak just fifty feet away provided the quick access hens seem to prefer, and just beyond that, a partially grown up field offered plenty of insects for the young poults. Bauer picked up a broken shell to show how the chick had pipped its circumference during hatching. A predator would have smashed the eggs into random fragments. A little farther down the road, we picked up the hen's signal. Bauer used his wrist-mounted GPS unit to pinpoint a location he could later transfer to a habitat map on his office computer. If any pattern emerges on what habitats turkey nesting hens prefer, property owners could manage for more of such habitat and increase nesting success and recruitment into the huntable population.

We finished up the morning by tracking another hen that Bauer thought might have successfully hatched poults before predators, possibly stray dogs, had destroyed the nest. However, he wanted to see the hen with the poults to know for sure if the nest had hatched successfully. We drove off into a narrow road that led to a one-acre food plot. Here, we got a strong signal. With the directional antenna, we followed the signal into a somewhat wet, grassy area, supporting a little clump of lizard tail with dropping white blooms. We climbed and stumbled over downed tree trunks and large limbs among scattered tall red oaks. A summer tanager called, "pick-a-tuck," and a male blue grosbeak sang from a high perch.

"We're real close," Bauer whispered, as we strained to see any sort of movement among the grass and limb debris ahead. Suddenly, a turkey flushed from thirty feet up in an oak and, with a rustling of flight feathers, flew strongly to the south and out of sight. Neither of us had anticipated a bird thirty feet up in a tree, certainly not in late morning. Nor had we seen any sign of poults, which cannot fly until they reach about two weeks old.

Bauer had further disappointing evidence indicating that perhaps predators had indeed gotten that hen's nest before the eggs had hatched.

As we returned to the office, Bauer admitted that this small sampling of the turkey nesting effort (he had found only two successful nests in this second year of the study) and the wide variety of habitats available might not yield any significant result; still, it represented a start. When I talked to Bauer a couple months later, he said that of the radio-tagged hens he had followed, half had initiated nesting and, of these ten nests, two had hatched successfully. He considered a 20 percent success rate pretty good. Of the failed nests, hens abandoned five and three succumbed to predators. By late July, when the poults have developed the capability of flight, successful hens again will gather into flocks with the youngsters following along.

Early summer finds another quite different but equally significant ACE breeding species. White shrimp, the mainstay of South Carolina's commercial and recreational harvest, spawn just offshore in May and June. As the eggs hatch, this new generation of shrimp rides the incoming tides into St. Helena Sound as two-week-old postlarvae and proceeds to the head of the smallest estuarine creeks. As summer progresses, the shrimp grow and mature into adults, feeding on the rich detrital soup of the salt marsh. They gradually work their way down the creeks, into the sound and eventually

In most years, white shrimp constitute the majority of South Carolina's commercial and recreational harvest. *Phillip Jones.*

seaward, seeking higher salinity water as they increase in size. By late August, most have moved to the deeper waters of the sound or just offshore.

If heavy rains keep salinity low in the sound, the shrimp migrate to offshore waters and into the commercial trawling area. However, a late summer with little rainfall keeps salinity high in the sound, and most white shrimp stay right there rather than moving offshore. In those years, recreational shrimpers, who work the shallow inshore waters with cast nets, enjoy a banner catch during the September to November shrimp-baiting season. The combination of this considerable fishing pressure, both commercial and recreational, appears to have little impact on the overall shrimp population, which fluctuates annually based almost entirely on environmental conditions.

The waters of St. Helen Sound and its surrounding creeks and rivers also provide ideal habitat for blue crabs, which support extensive commercial and recreational fisheries. Unlike shrimp, crabs have a protracted spawning period from February to November with peaks in late spring and again in fall. Females mate while soft following their final molt. After the new shell hardens, they move to just offshore to spawn, carrying the yellow egg mass under their abdomen. The eggs hatch in about two weeks, and the larvae migrate into the estuaries seeking the small creeks where, like so many other local marine animals, they find abundant nutrients and some protection from predators as they grow and develop. Juvenile crabs produced in the spring spawn populate the marsh creeks abundantly throughout the summer.

The flooding of the ACE Basin's many managed impoundments along the tidal creeks and rivers pulls in shrimp and crabs as well as numerous species of estuarine fishes, trapping them in these enclosed wetlands, which interrupts their normal life cycles and removes them from the public domain. Many property managers draw down impoundment water levels in the spring to expose mud flats for migrating shorebirds. When the shorebirds move on, reflooding the ponds encourages native plants such as widgeon grass and dwarf spike rush, relished by wintering waterfowl. This incoming flow from estuarine waters brings with it countless larval shrimp, crabs and juvenile fish of many species.

Once into the impoundments, only a small percentage of these organisms ever escape back into the creek. The rest provide food for avian predators or succumb to the stress of extreme temperatures and low dissolved oxygen that often characterize impoundment waters. Midsummer drawdowns and subsequent reflooding of impoundments can heavily recruit larval brown shrimp, for example, which usually abound in the creeks at that time of year. Studies show that less than 8 percent of these shrimp entrained into impoundments ever escape. Midsummer water exchange also pulls in large numbers of larval ladyfish, tarpon and croaker. Larval spot, on the other hand, not abundant during midsummer, may enter impoundments at other times of the year. This seasonal selection results in a species composition of fishes in impoundments quite different from that in the unaltered creeks. Researchers have found mummichogs the most abundant fish in the creeks while mosquito fish top the list of impoundment fishes. One study noted sixteen more species of fishes in the creeks than in impounded wetlands.

One hot, late June morning, Bear Island WMA manager Ross Catterton invited me to join him to check on an extensive impoundment known as Lower Pine. A couple days earlier, he had adjusted the doors of the trunks that control water levels in Lower Pine so that water drained from the field at every low tide but did not reenter at high tide.

"I was about to lose this pond," he explained as we rode an ATV along the perimeter dike. Widgeon grass, the species he targeted here, will grow up to two feet in length if provided with enough water depth, but the topography of this pond limits the maximum depth to just ten or twelve inches. The topped-out grass had started to decay, providing a platform for an algal bloom. Left unchecked, the algae would shade out the widgeon grass, killing it and causing the loss of the pond as a producer of waterfowl food for the season. Draining the pond destroyed the algae and allowed the widgeon grass to reseed and start a second crop. A new crop of widgeon grass had just started on the exposed muddy substrate that had baked in the sun for a few days. Ross also pointed with satisfaction to a faint blush of green indicating dwarf spike rush had also made a fresh start on the mud flats among the thick stands of salt marsh bulrush unfazed by the drawdown. In ponds of lower salinity where Ross targets primarily dwarf spike rush, he attempts to eliminate problem algae by lowering the water level to just a few inches but not drying the substrate completely. This gives the spike rush a better chance to recover. By lowering the water level in Bear Island's twenty-eight ponds in a staggered schedule, the new crops of duck food become available at different times throughout the fall as various species arrive during the prolonged fall migration. Wading birds also benefit whenever shallow water concentrates fish and other prey species.

Managers such as Catterton adjust water levels during much of the year to provide the optimal amount of food for the waterfowl that will winter in these ponds. As with most habitat management, the goal becomes the interruption of plant succession. In this case, that means preventing the takeover of the emergent vegetation typical of the salt marsh, primarily spartina, to allow the dominance of early successional species, such as widgeon grass. The addition of brackish water to raise the salinity also controls freshwater emergents, such as the undesirable cattails, which have no wildlife food value. Impoundment managers thus have two tools they can use to alter plant succession: the manipulation of water levels and, in many ponds, the ability to change salinity by flooding ponds from different water sources or with varying salinities depending on tidal stage and rainfall.

In the quest to manage impoundments for wintering waterfowl, salt marsh fauna—including fishes, shrimp and crabs—simply become collateral damage and turn impoundments into giant bird feeders. Ross and I saw an example of this later the same morning as we drove along the upper dike of Bear Island's "house pond" at the property entrance. Ross had pulled down the water in this pond for the same reason: to start another crop of widgeon grass and spike rush. Here, a few inches of water remained in some low spots, greatly concentrating the surviving aquatic organisms. Hundreds of egrets, herons, wood storks and a single roseate spoonbill joined about fifty white pelicans in a feeding frenzy.

State law, enacted decades ago, prohibited the construction of new impoundments, based on their adverse impact on natural salt marsh production. Under current law, property owners can repair existing dikes but cannot build new dikes or impound open marshes or swamps. The ACE Basin's core area contains twenty-six thousand acres of impoundments, most of those managed for waterfowl, shorebirds and wading birds. How property owners manage these wetlands and how they time drawdowns and reflooding has a huge impact on the ecology of the entire area. Typical management practices benefit a variety of waterfowl, wading birds and shorebirds, along with bald eagles, ospreys and other water birds.

Simple wooden water control structures, called rice field trunks, make it possible to carefully manipulate water levels. Trunks (the earliest just that: hollowed-out tree trunks) consist of a wooden tunnel, usually thirty-two feet long, five feet wide and eighteen inches high on the inside. Buried under a dike, a trunk allows water to pass back and forth from a tidal creek to an impoundment with the flow rate controlled by doors held by uprights at each end of the trunk. Opening the door on the creek side floods the impoundment on the rising tide, and opening the door on the impoundment side of the dike allows water to drain on a falling tide.

Rice planters in the ACE Basin and other parts of the Southeast coast first used this structure to control water levels during the rice culture's 150-year reign along the area's tidal rivers. Since the commercially grown rice

Rice planters, using slaves and mules, dug the seven-mile-long Mathewes Canal on Bear Island WMA to channel fresh water to rice fields. *Pete Laurie.*

could not tolerate salt, the planters cleared the marshes and wooded swamps along the freshwater tidal stretches of the Ashepoo, Combahee and Edisto Rivers. Coastal South Carolina's tidal range of six feet or more, even well inland from the ocean, allowed for the conversion of thousands of acres of riverfront land into rice fields.

The considerable freshwater flow of the extensive Edisto and Combahee River systems allowed rice cultivation to flourish well downriver. Meanwhile, the large tidal range and the general low topography pushes the tidal influence far inland beyond the reach of salt water, perhaps the key characteristic of this unique geographical area. The Edisto, Ashepoo and Combahee all experience considerable tidal fluctuation well west of U.S. Highway 17. This predictable daily rise and fall of river levels well inland from the reach of salt water allowed rice planters to flood and drain their fields as needed with the fresh water that rice requires.

With the demise of rice planting in the early 1900s, northerners bought up many of the old plantations and converted them to hunting preserves, using the existing dikes and trunks to manage the abandoned rice fields to grow native plants that attract wintering waterfowl. Many of these plants do better in brackish water, which changes the management scheme somewhat but not the use of trunks, a design basically unchanged for three hundred years, except for the addition of a spillway box that allows excess rainwater to drain from the impoundment without adjusting the doors. Otherwise, only construction materials have changed—from cypress originally, to creosoted pine and finally today to pine treated with chromated copper arsenic. In addition, stainless steel nails and bolts have replaced the wooden pegs once used to hold trunks together. Even with modern treated lumber and stainless steel fasteners, trunks last only twenty to forty years before some combination of decay and wood borers eventually causes them to fail. Properties with many acres of wetlands have to constantly build new trunks to replace the failing ones. In general, one trunk will serve one hundred acres of wetland, but this can vary with the layout of the impoundments and the available sources of tidally driven water. Bear Island, for example, has about ninety trunks, which Ross and his staff check almost daily, adjusting the doors or spillway boxes as necessary to maintain ideal water levels.

Trunk building requires precision and attention to detail. A poorly constructed trunk seldom works properly. Installing a replacement trunk usually requires the digging of a new hole adjacent to the old trunk. The bottom of the hole must correspond precisely with the low tide mark, with the trunk set exactly level and in several inches of mud to prevent water from leaking under the structure. Modern track hoes and other heavy equipment take much of the labor out of trunk installation. Before such conveniences, workers (slaves prior to 1863) built trunks close to the dikes and floated them into place at high tide. After properly placing the trunk, workers today drive heavy wooden sheeting into the ground to hold the rebuilt dike in place. They then bury the old trunk and alter the creek or canal that serves the replacement trunk.

Ross stopped the ATV at a recently replaced trunk that moved water from the needle rush marsh along the Ashepoo River into the impoundment called Sara, which he decided needed a little more water. With a long steel bar he pried up the tidal side door a few inches. Holding the bar down with his foot, he removed the two pins that hold the door in place and moved them up two holes. Stepping off the bar, he allowed the door to drop just slightly so that it rested about four inches higher than before. This let in a greater flow of water on each high tide, increasing the water depth after a few tidal cycles. Gradually adding water to increase growth of waterfowl plants in managed impoundments becomes a regular summertime activity at many ACE Basin properties.

A sprinkler keeps the boards from shrinking on a just completed trunk as it awaits installation. *Pete Laurie.*

By midsummer, activity at the Donnelley WMA wading bird rookery had declined dramatically. Spring's busy comings and goings of adult birds bringing food to nestlings had slowed to just a few wood storks and anhinga soaring over head. Wood stork chicks, by now almost the size of their parents,

Wood storks fly as far as twenty miles from their nesting rookeries to forage and then return to regurgitate food for their chicks. *Phillip Jones.*

Little blue herons nest in colonies, often with other wading birds. *Phillip Jones.*

stood idly on their stick platforms, appearing all but ready to leave their nests, where they spend up to fifty-five days before developing the necessary feathers and wing power to fly. Little blue heron chicks, also the size of adults but sporting the white plumage of their youth, seemed equally anxious to fledge and get on with the business of life as a few blue-gray adults stepped among the branches that support the now well-worn nests.

A little farther downstream in this old inland rice system, a few pairs of red-winged blackbirds still demonstrated breeding behavior as their nesting season approached completion for another year. Here, water lotus, one of the myriad plants that inhabit freshwater wetlands, had erupted into large, showy yellow blooms that would eventually fade into distinctive disk-shaped seedpods. Much of the pickerelweed and arrowhead had finished blooming, although both of these common freshwater wetland species have long flowering seasons that linger into October. Bird song also had mostly ended for the year, although a male painted bunting sang his whistled territorial song from a little live oak at the dike's edge. Painted buntings often produce three and sometimes four broods per year, so nesting continues long after most other songbirds have finished for the season. At the end of the dike, a much less locally common indigo bunting male tended to an active brood of four fledglings, his iridescent plumage much in contrast with the dull brown of the youngsters. Indigo buntings raise just one or two broods per year and so complete their breeding season much sooner.

A week later, still just mid-July, I saw the first sign of fall migration: several hundred rough-winged swallows massed on the power lines where Bennetts Point Road crosses Fee Farm Creek. These swallows nest in holes that they excavate in the banks of streams, or sometimes, they use holes in masonry walls and protruding pipes, of which the ACE Basin has little. Most rough wings fly farther north or inland to nest. Like indigo buntings, rough-winged swallows raise only one brood and have finished breeding by the middle of summer. I perhaps had seen these very same birds just eight or nine weeks ago on the power line going into Bear Island, although this species continues to migrate through the area well into the fall as nesting birds from the northern part of their range make their way south in similar large flocks on their way to the wintering grounds in Central America.

Ignoring these few early hints of fall, I took advantage of a beautiful summer day to get a firsthand look at a water quality–monitoring program in the Edisto River. From its inception in 1992, the National Estuarine Research Reserve has conducted an ongoing water quality assessment program in the wetlands associated with the three rivers and where they meet at St. Helena Sound. DNR biologist Chuck Tucker and intern Rachael Kassabian invited me to go along on their monthly trip to change out sophisticated data recorders at seven monitoring stations in the South Edisto River. First put in place twenty years ago, these deceptively simple-looking cylinders, three inches in diameter and about two feet long, take readings of temperature, salinity, pH, dissolved oxygen, turbidity and water depth every fifteen minutes, 365 days per year.

We left Bennetts Point in an eighteen-foot outboard boat late on a hot, humid midweek morning. With Tucker at the helm, the 115-horsepower engine eased us down Mosquito Creek past the docks, and then as Tucker pushed the throttle forward, we got up to speed as we approached the Ashepoo River. Turning downstream, we soon entered the Intracoastal Waterway (ICW), and shortly after that, we reached Fenwick Cut, which in 1904 split Fenwick Island in two. Seconds later, we sped into the South Edisto and continued downstream, the beach houses and condos on the backside of Edisto Island just specks on the southern horizon. A family of bottlenose dolphins arched at the surface, the explosive "woosh" as they exhaled drowned by the whining engine as we skimmed past.

Vacationers with hand lines and dip nets worked the Edisto back beach for blue crabs as we turned at the river's mouth into Big Bay Creek and, obeying the "No Wake" signs, idled slowly past new-looking beach homes, each with an expensive boat tied to a dock. One of the very few populated parts of the ACE Basin, Edisto Beach seemed quiet on a weekday, but this creek no doubt comes to life on summer weekends with plenty of boat traffic, a key factor in selecting one of these docks as a site for a data recorder. Kassabian and I held the boat against the dock as Tucker fished the device out of its protective PVC sleeve and replaced it with a fresh one. He said that to the surprise of researchers, only salinity varied much between this station and the other stations in areas with little direct human impact or boat traffic.

At our next stop, close by on the DNR dock, at the ACE Basin Visitors' Center, Tucker proudly showed off a satellite uplink system he had recently installed. Once completely up and running, this station will transmit the data directly to the NERR office computer. However, as he explained, he would still have to change out the data recorder monthly to remove oysters, barnacles and other fouling organisms. We then wound our way northward through a maze of marsh creeks, narrowed by the falling tide. In the completely drained feeder creeks, bristling mounds of oyster bars sat high and dry. Clapper rails, startled by the sudden approach of the boat,

Twice daily, meandering creeks flood and drain the ACE Basin's extensive salt marshes.
Phillip Jones.

protested loudly from the thick stands of spartina that towered above us. Black-bellied plovers and whimbrels flushed ahead of us, twisting along the course of the creeks as they threaded their way through the grassy maze. The whimbrels had probably already completed their short breeding season in the far north and had begun their long migration to the South American wintering grounds. Soon, we turned into the wider expanse of St. Pierre

Creek where Tucker had another station, this one in a narrow feeder creek just one hundred yards or so off the main channel.

"This one sometimes has toad fish in it," he said, gingerly pulling the data recorder from the PVC. "I even found a stone crab in this pipe one time," he added. I held the boat steady against the post while Tucker and Kassabian made the quick exchange of devices, the spartina all around us lush and green in the summer sun. Just below the surface of the murky water, a blue crab sculled past the boat, a reminder of the unseen aquatic life all around us. These meandering creeks, in all their countless miles that twice daily flood and drain the ACE Basin's salt marshes, support the larval and juvenile stages of 75 percent of the seafood harvested along the coast. In midsummer, juvenile white shrimp probably surrounded our boat. By fall, these shrimp, as adults, will move into deeper waters of the sound where cast netters working at night will fill their coolers and the commercial trawlers will catch them by the boxful just offshore. Here, too, larval seatrout, juvenile red drum and many other fishes find abundant food and some refuge from predators as they grow and mature.

All these marsh animals of course have their own internal data recorders, equally sensitive to changes in salinity, pH, temperature, turbidity, dissolved oxygen—all the parameters the expensive man-made devices can record—and the crabs, shrimp and fishes at least have the ability to move from stressful conditions to more favorable locales. Less mobile organisms shut themselves into shells or burrow into the mud when conditions become intolerable. As Tucker slid the replacement data recorder into the pipe, the tide here had just started to turn. Herds of fiddler crabs climbed the steep pluff mud banks toward their burrows, and a mullet jumped just ahead of the boat as we eased back into the broader waters of St. Pierre Creek. From the perspective of the boat on the water's surface, such casual glimpses of marsh animals belie the reality of the myriad and vibrant life below with all its frantic interplay of predator and prey.

"We've got about a thirty-minute run to our next station," Tucker said, turning over the helm to Kassabian as we headed up the South Edisto, wide and calm near its mouth, the marsh edge now just a distant green line between the water and a fleet of cumulus clouds stretching across the horizon. Of all the measurements the data recorders collect, researchers have the most interest in the salinity gradient of the river from the beach up to the freshwater/saltwater dividing line. As sea levels rise with climate change, salinity pushes farther and farther inland on the ACE's tidal rivers and all streams flowing into estuaries around the world. Short-term changes,

Brown pelicans, common summer residents in the ACE Basin, have made an excellent comeback after pesticides decimated their population in the 1960s. *Phillip Jones.*

however, often mask longer-term trends. In 2013, for example, a year of considerable rainfall, all seven stations in this study had lower salinities than the previous five years, when the state suffered a prolonged drought.

The ICW runs through this stretch of the river, and with the low tide following us upstream, Kassabian kept the boat close to the channel markers, avoiding the hidden shallows and large mud flats just barely exposed in the middle of the river. On the north bank, mounds of washed shell, pushed up by the wakes of large vessels, shone white against the green of the marsh grass. Following the markers, we abruptly turned east into Watts Cut, another man-made part of the ICW, here connecting the South Edisto with the Dawhoo River, which eventually joins the Wadmalaw River to form the North Edisto. This cut runs straight for more than one mile before merging with North Creek, a tributary of the Dawhoo. A large, well-supported pipe projecting from the brushy edge suggested a dredge spoil area just beyond the dike, although a lack of funding has so reduced dredging that parts of the waterway have become choked with silt and difficult to navigate even at high tide. Soon, the towering Dawhoo River Bridge loomed ahead, but just before reaching it, we swung north into the river, and after a few bends, we branched off into Fishing Creek, one of a number of waterways in the ACE with this name. Still at full throttle, we snaked our way deep into the marsh, the creek narrowing with every tight turn, until we reached a solitary post supporting another data recorder.

Tucker explained that researchers initially selected this remote spot as a control for sites in areas of higher boat traffic and other human influences. However, over the years, most data here have varied little from the first site we visited on populated Big Bay Creek behind Edisto Beach. However, now a good fifteen river miles inland, the salinity at this spot varies from zero to eighteen parts per thousand depending mostly on rainfall. Despite the widely fluctuating salinity, vegetation remained very much salt marsh with tall, vibrant green spartina soaring well above us in the boat. Clumps of mud and growing grass slumped into the water where the current undercut the soft substrate. With the recording devices quickly exchanged, we retraced our route back past the bridge, through Watts Cut again, and continued up the Edisto as it makes a long horseshoe curve around Jehossee Island, part of the Hollings National Wildlife Refuge. Scores of laughing gulls resting on an exposed sandbar watched us skim past, the river still wide as we raced upstream.

The refuge dock on the Charleston County side of the Edisto supported our next station. Small live oaks and red cedars had started to replace the spartina on the river's edge, and eroded clumps of pickerelweed and arrowhead floated on the current, all signs we had transitioned from brackish water to fresh. A mile or so farther upriver, we reached our most inland station on a solitary post near the bank at the northern edge of the refuge. An ancient stump of oak or cedar, just barely exposed by the tide, suggested a once lower river level many years ago. A small gator showed just its eyes and nose in the shallows as a male painted bunting chased a female in the shrubby groundsel trees on the bank. Salinity at this station, Tucker said, never registered more than a fraction of a point above zero. Still, the area experienced a tidal range of several feet or more judging by the high-water mark.

Hundreds of years ago, rice planters sought out just these sections of the ACE Basin's rivers: above the reach of salt yet with enough difference between high and low tide to flood and drain the fields as needed to produce the famous Carolina Gold. In the one hundred years since the demise of the rice culture, and with rising sea levels, these areas of tidal fresh water have no doubt moved inland. Now rising at an accelerated pace due to climate change, the increased sea level has no doubt pushed salt water farther and farther upstream with the tidal areas of the Ashepoo, Combahee and Edisto undergoing major changes in both flora and fauna. The various "cuts" made during construction of the Intracoastal Waterway also altered the salinity profiles in these rivers. The water quality data collected now will serve as benchmarks to document these changes in future years.

Having traversed the entire stretch of the brackish portion of the South Edisto, about thirty river miles, Kassabian nosed the boat around, and we headed back downstream, the incoming tide and slight onshore breeze stirring up a washboard chop. We passed a single yacht heading north on the ICW, but otherwise, we had the river to ourselves before slicing again through Fenwick Cut and back into the Ashepoo, which we soon left, as the waterway turned south. In a few more minutes, we approached the DNR dock at Bennetts Point. For Chuck Tucker, the trip ended with mixed emotions. After two and a half years, he had just made his last of these monthly runs, having decided to take a job teaching high school science. "I'm going to miss these river trips," he said, gazing across the marsh. "But not all the hours in the office compiling the data."

A couple weeks later, I took another boat ride in the NERR, checking this time on migrating shorebirds. We think of fall as a time of bird migration, but for many shorebirds, some of which make long trips from the northern nesting grounds to the farthest reaches of South America, the annual southern trek begins in midsummer. The ACE Basin offers many places for these migrants to rest and refuel, just as it does during the spring migration for these same shorebirds. The front beach of uninhabited Otter Island provides one such key resting area, and on the last day of July, Nick Wallover and I took the short boat ride from Bennetts Point out to the north end of Otter to take a look. Nick, the field station manager for the NERR, regularly visited Otter and, with the tide near high and rising, took us through a shortcut from the South Edisto to the island's north end. He steered the boat into a little cut through the marsh that connected to another of the many Fishing Creeks in the ACE. This creek hugs the wooded edge of South Fenwick Island and then strikes out across the marshes that separate South Fenwick and Pine Islands, terminating at the inlet between Pine and Otter.

We beached the boat where the sands of Otter curve around to a small high spot of stunted red cedars. Eroding into a spartina-lined slough, this narrow strip of sand sported clumps of Russian thistle, or saltwort. As we walked along the inlet, beach hoppers skipped from underfoot. A flock of laughing gulls and windswept-looking royal terns stood facing the onshore breeze. Dark summer shower clouds hung on the horizon just offshore. Otter's north end consists of a narrow, eroding strip of beach backed by

THE ACE BASIN

Migrating earlier through the ACE Basin than in past years, marbled godwits stand at the edge of the Otter Island surf in August. *Phillip Jones.*

acres of salt marsh dotted with small, wooded hummocks. At one slightly higher spot on the beach, a few red cedars clung to existence, and a salt marsh skipper probed the yellow bloom of a sea ox-eye. Where the beach swept southward, we could see in the distance dark clumps of resting birds, still too far off to identify even with binoculars. As we approached, though, we began to discern a great variety of birds of all sizes resting on this remote beach. Among the low dunes, the smaller shorebirds—semi-palmated plovers, western sandpipers and semi-palmated sandpipers, all early migrants—mixed with a few sanderlings, a couple of the males still in the breeding plumage of rusty-colored head and neck. Just a few weeks earlier, Nick had seen far fewer shorebirds here. The fall migration clearly had begun.

At the high tide mark, eight or ten willets, all black and white in flight, took to the air, calling a strident, "Pill-will-it." But of more interest, a dark, tightly bunched flock of marbled godwits stood close to the surf, surrounded by brown pelicans, royal terns, least terns and laughing gulls. One of North America's largest shorebirds, marbled godwits, with their buffy-brown plumage and long, upturned bills, once passed through South Carolina much later, primarily from September to November, according to accounts of that time. Yet here we watched them at the end of July and not just a few early wanderers—at least fifty. These birds had no doubt completed nesting on the grasslands of western Canada and, with no reason to linger in the north, had already made a good start on their

During the day, ghost crabs stay close to their burrows on the beach at Botany Bay WMA. *Phillip Jones.*

return journey to the south. A few might spend the winter locally, but most would continue on to the coast of Guatemala and even Ecuador, where they would remain until next spring. Marbled godwits consume insects on their nesting grounds, but on migration, they probe the mud flats for marine worms, small crustaceans and mollusks. With the high tide covering these productive feeding areas, the godwits seemed content to simply stand on the beach, staring out to sea. This flock, the vanguard of many more to come, perhaps will linger in the ACE Basin for a few days to fuel up before continuing south. Once considered a game bird and decimated by overhunting, marbled godwits, now fully protected, have returned to something approaching their historic numbers.

Among this concentration of local birds and migrants, we noted another traveler, this one not unexpected by late July. A single black tern, still in its dark breeding plumage, stood out among the predominantly white gulls and other terns. Like the godwits, black terns nest on the prairies but migrate along the East Coast, arriving in the ACE Basin in late summer. They often quickly pass through, as some winter as far south as Chile. A freshwater species on its breeding grounds, black terns migrate close to the coast, feeding on small fishes, and generally do not stay long, making them easily overlooked in some years. Because birdwatchers and scientists usually spot black terns in flocks, this single bird on the beach seemed quite out of place. A few weeks later, I watched a dozen swooping over Bear Island's impoundments.

Leaving the birds on the beach undisturbed, we retracted our steps, noting the small yellow signs that advised visitors to stay out of the sparse patches of sea oats and silver leaf croton in the low dunes where least terns often nest. Nick said these smallest of the local terns had not nested on Otter for two years, and that earlier in the summer he had located only a dozen nests of Wilson plovers. Such variations in short-term nesting behavior involve many factors and may not have long-term consequences. As the tide retreated, we noted that the Otter Island beach contained the remains of a few long-dead horseshoe crabs but very few shells of whelks and other mollusks so common on Botany Bay just a few miles north.

Returning to the boat, Nick ignored the ominous clouds and decided to navigate across the front of Pine Island to get back into the South Edisto. He steered us through the choppy inlet into the ocean and then north, staying between the breakers on the sandbar a couple hundred yards offshore and the marshy fringe off the island. The confused seas with four-foot swells from various angles bounced us around while Nick paid close attention to the depth gauge. Gradually, we approached the distant shoreline on the south end of Edisto Beach until we could see vacationers in the surf. Suddenly, the water depth dropped from ten to thirty feet as we entered the river channel near its mouth. We headed upriver as the waves subsided and Nick pushed the throttle forward. We raced toward Bennetts Point, black clouds surrounding us the whole way back to the dock. We beat the rain by minutes.

A week later, I stumbled onto a quite different concentration of birds at a drawdown in the lower pond of the Donnelley WMA old rice field complex. Several trunks control the water levels here, and all had their inside doors raised and their outside doors closed to the Old Chehaw River. With the doors in this position for the last several days, each low tide had drained this extensive wetland, but the lowered outside doors had blocked the inflow from the river on high tide. As a result, just a few inches of water remained on the bed of the pond, with more water in the deeper canal along Fishburne Bank. Left with only shallow water or crowded into the deeper canal, fish struggled to survive. To complicate the situation, several overcast days had reduced algal photosynthesis, the byproduct of which replenishes the vitally important dissolved oxygen in the water. Heavy showers had added rainwater, which contains no dissolved oxygen, further stressing aquatic life.

With dissolved oxygen so low, thousands of small fish, their mouths open, gasped for air at the surface. Many had already died and washed up to the edge of the steep bank. Their light color, forked tail and vertical dark bars identified them as spot, a common estuarine species. Incoming water during

Summer drawdowns in impoundments concentrate fish and invertebrates, making them easy prey for wading birds and alligators. *Pete Laurie.*

the last flooding of this pond had no doubt swept in the larvae of these now three- to four-inch fish. While the water level remained at twelve to fifteen inches, they had survived and grown, but now they had suddenly run out of water and with it the life-giving oxygen. The greatly stressed fish had not gone unnoticed by predatory birds. The entire pond had turned white as hundreds of great egrets, snowy egrets and wood storks stalked the shallow water among flocks of white pelicans while laughing gulls and Caspian terns wheeled overhead, all feeding on the dying fish. Yellowlegs, willets and black-necked stilts patrolled the wet edges, probing the mud for invertebrates suddenly accessible to the birds' long bills. Ten roseate spoonbills added a festive touch of pink to the gathering.

The shallow water had also forced the pond's considerable alligator population into the deeper water along the dike. Here, they enjoyed a fish feast, as they thrashed at the surface, often with a large mullet visible in their long, toothy jaws. Within an area of just a couple hundred or so square yards, I counted fifty gators, just their eyes and noses exposed as they floated at the surface. Managed wetlands in the ACE support an estimated one alligator per acre, but it takes a concentration such as this to appreciate just how many gators ply these shallow wetlands. In fact, this impressive concentration of birds and gators underscored the productivity of impoundments and brought into focus how man's manipulation of natural habitats can favor certain species, in this case the birds and gators, to the detriment of other species, here the fish and aquatic invertebrates.

Summer fish kills, such as the one I witnessed, occur regularly in impoundments when the combination of high temperature, several overcast days and heavy rainfall combine to reduce the amount of dissolved oxygen in these shallow wetlands. However, many such kills take place just at dawn after hours of darkness with no photosynthesis. Within a few hours of daylight, the birds and alligators often have consumed the dead and dying fish, and the kill goes unnoticed.

Only a few resident hawks spend the summer in the ACE Basin. Red-tailed hawks nest throughout the area near open areas and scattered woodlands, where they feed on rabbits and small mammals, such as cotton and rice rats. They commonly hunt from exposed perches and often soar overhead with shrill, hoarse cries. The related red-shouldered hawk prefers wooded swamps where it preys on frogs, snakes and occasionally crawfish, in addition to some rodents. Its strident calls, repeated up to a dozen times, resemble those of a blue jay. Much less common, Cooper's hawks haunt thick cover, where they ambush songbirds and, on occasion, mourning doves and quail. The populations of all three species see an increase in fall and winter as northern ranging birds drift south after the breeding season. A mostly summer raptor, the osprey, nests throughout the ACE in tall dead trees, on navigational markers and on man-made platforms, finding plenty of fish to eat in the area's extensive wetlands. Common winter raptors, including bald eagles, sharp-shinned hawks, harriers and all three eastern North American falcons—kestrel, merlin and peregrine—vanish for the summer. Having completed their prolonged nesting season, eagles leave in late May to spend the summer in the Chesapeake Bay, the Great Lakes region and farther north.

For coldblooded reptiles and amphibians, summer's warm weather allows greater activity, but the leafy vegetative growth of the season makes them difficult to see. Many amphibians prefer small, isolated wetlands that occasionally go dry during the summer. Both frogs and salamanders avoid wetlands that support fish, which prey heavily on both adults and juveniles amphibians. To evade these predators, many frogs and salamanders seek out small wet spots that periodically dry out completely, precluding fish. The amphibians have adapted to survive prolonged droughts by burrowing into the mud, where they remain completely torpid for weeks. The ACE Basin abounds in small isolated wetlands—Donnelley Wildlife Management

Area's eight thousand acres, for example, contain more than 150 such small wet spots, including old sloughs and partially filled-in drains, as well as depression meadows, low spots with clay soil and no source of water other than rainfall. Since fires regularly burn through the depression meadows, woody plants seldom become established, allowing grasses and herbaceous plants to dominate.

The isolated wetlands formed in old sloughs often include small hardwoods, especially black gum and live oak. These low spots may hold water for much of the year, becoming "gator holes" where a single alligator sets up an isolated residence, subsisting on frogs, snakes and turtles, as well as raccoons, possums, deer and other mammals that pause to drink. Just a few square feet at the surface, such holes may exceed six feet or more in depth. Cloudy water indicates a gator "at home," while clear water suggests the gator may have temporarily moved to another nearby wet spot. Approaching one of these isolated wetlands in summer usually triggers a flurry of frog activity with leopard frogs vaulting with long graceful leaps into the surrounding grass, bullfrogs splashing across the surface and the startled "squeenk" of green frogs. Frogs and toads, of which the ACE Basin contains twenty-one species, make a variety of

Bits of duckweed cling to a cottonmouth water moccasin, just emerged from an old rice reserve. *Pete Laurie.*

croaks, squeaks and snores. The silent, secretive salamanders (sixteen species in the ACE) remain all but unknown to most people.

Many reptiles, especially snakes, also seek out very specific habitats, with stump holes prized for denning during the winter and ideal for avoiding the heat of summer days. As tree stumps rot, they leave behind holes that may stretch many feet into the ground, both vertically and horizontally. These stump holes provide perfect burrows for lizards and snakes, most of which go into a state of lower metabolism during the winter. After emerging in the spring, snakes may require up to eight weeks of basking in the sun to regain full activity. While most snakes seem to prefer the stump holes left by pines, very small holes have little value. Areas managed for the production of pulpwood, with the trees harvested every fifteen to twenty years, never develop any large stump holes and, therefore, support fewer snakes.

Summer's waning days bring a flurry of yellow blooming wildflowers. In upland areas, partridge pea, a tall, branched annual, and the naturalized (and toxic) rattlebox, along with goldenrod of several species, cover edges and disturbed areas with a yellow wash. By late summer, several related species of seed box, all members of the evening primrose family, bloom along the edges of wetlands, producing creamy flowers of four to seven petals. Less common in local wetlands, giant yellow-eyed grass develops tiny flowers all but hidden in woody knobs atop narrow, four-foot-tall stems. One mid-August morning, I stumbled onto a lesser-seen yellow flower, the crested fringed orchid, blooming in some open pinewoods. Along with the seasonal yellow, a little red also begins to creep into the foliage at this time of year, with black gums and Virginia creeper showing a scarlet leaf here and there.

With summer just starting to fade, but still very much in evidence, deer hunting begins on private land in the ACE Basin on August 15 each year and runs through the end of December, one of the longest deer seasons in the country. By mid-August, many bucks still sport velvet on their antlers, and a few late season fawns still retain their spots, none of which deters some hunters. However, with such a long season and with August usually hot and humid, many hunters wait until September or October to begin hunting. Up until recent decades, local hunters used dogs to flush deer from cover. Today, though, must hunters have discovered they have greater success still hunting from tree stands, without the expense and complications of maintaining a pack of deerhounds.

Before the passage of hunting regulations in the 1920s and 1930s, deer populations declined to the point that very little deer hunting took place in South Carolina, and that only in the thickly forested coastal swamps.

Restocking programs, begun in the 1950s, along with better management practices, changes in land uses and more diligent law enforcement, have now increased deer numbers across the state until they have become a problem for farmers and a nuisance in residential neighborhoods. The extensive upland forests of the ACE Basin provide ideal habitat that supports a healthy population of white-tailed deer. The widespread practice of controlled burns in the pinewoods ensures plenty of young, tender shoots, the browse deer prefer. Deer also feed on corn and other agricultural crops, as well as in isolated food plots planted for wildlife. As with many mammals with an extensive north-to-south range, white-tailed deer follow Bergmann's rule, which states that smaller individuals of the species inhabit the more southern parts of the range. ACE Basin white-tailed bucks seldom exceed two hundred pounds, much smaller than bucks of the same species roaming the woods of northern Michigan.

The early start of deer season signals the beginning of the fall hunts for doves, quail, squirrels, rabbits, raccoons and, of course, ducks. The popularity of sport hunting has driven the management of both public and private uplands and wetlands throughout the ACE since the demise of rice production. Hunting has a direct positive economic impact on the ACE Basin. Some landowners lease the deer hunting rights to local hunt clubs, a source of revenue that helps pay the taxes on the property and allows them to keep large holdings intact. Revenues from license sales and from the federal excise tax on hunting equipment help pay for the management of public lands, which allow carefully controlled hunts for a variety of species. Non-game species of many types benefit directly or indirectly from all these management practices that target game species. If not for hunting, the old rice plantations might have fallen into ruin decades ago, losing much of their value to wildlife.

With Labor Day looming on the calendar, I made one last summertime trip to the ACE, deciding to cruise down State Highway 43 toward the little settlement of Dale on the Beaufort County side of the Combahee River. Similar to Bennetts Point Road and Wiggins Road, Highway 43 makes a long, tentative probe into the basin's wetlands until eventually running out of high ground. That these three roads never connect attests to the extent of the impassable marshes, creeks and rivers and helps explain how and why development has left the ACE pretty much as intact as when Europeans first settled the South Carolina coast. Before reaching Dale, I turned left onto a wide gravel road that led, straight as a string, to Wimbee Creek Landing. Here the road, which once served the old Seaboard Coast line that ran through Charleston and on to Savannah, ended at the remains of an old trestle. Concreted on top with a chain-link railing to either side, the remnants of the trestle now extend less than halfway across the wide creek, creating a fishing pier/observation deck.

To the east, the sun, partially shrouded by low clouds, had climbed just above the trees on North Williman Island as I walked out on the old trestle. The river stood at low slack water with a modern floating dock at the landing resting in the mud where a few laughing gulls, already in fall plumage, cackled loudly. Several rock doves, normally city dwellers, flew about the structure as a kingfisher rattled from a piling. A bottlenose dolphin swam under the trestle right beneath my feet, startling me with a sudden "whoosh" as it took a breath. The single animal moved easily through the turbid water, briefly investigated a small marsh drain, thought better of it and, with another explosive breath, continued downstream toward the confluence with Williman Creek at the head of Bull River.

With a light, misty fog rolling across the creek, a marsh hen, or clapper rail, stepped boldly from the thick spartina, glancing cautiously around, up to its ankles in the pluff mud on the creek bank. Closer to the water's edge, a much smaller spotted sandpiper pattered about, pausing to teeter back and forth before taking to the air. With fluttery, shallow wing beats as it called, "Pip, pip, pip," it flew low across the water in a long loop that brought it back to the bank fifty yards farther upstream. The spartina bordering the ramp had begun its fall bloom with many of the stalks sprouting long spikes of tiny straw-colored flowers, giving the marsh a lighter look. Above the high tide mark, green berries clung tightly to the branches of a yaupon holly. By winter, they would mature to a decorative bright red.

I drove back to Highway 17 and turned north across the Harriet Tubman Bridge over the Combahee. On the Charleston County side of the river, the great expanse of salt marsh shone with a wheat-like glow of thousands of seed heads topping the spartina stalks. I turned north on White Hall Road, a straight stretch of secondary road lined with large hardwoods. Oaks and hickories hung over the highway up past Cockfield Plantation and beyond to the turn off to Cuckhold's Creek Landing. Here, the tide still flowed smartly seaward, even though far downstream the incoming tide had already begun to surge up the lower Combahee system. Across this narrow creek, an immature Cooper's hawk suddenly swooped above the brackish wetland, chattering loudly as it chased a couple less-than-amused crows among the old cypress staubs.

Back on White Hall Road, I crossed the railroad tracks and eased past the plantation that gave the road its name. Behind the white board fence,

Spartina stalks in bloom impart a yellow hue to salt marshes in the early fall. *Pete Laurie.*

neatly mowed grass surrounded dozens of great spreading live oaks in front of the main house and outbuildings. Through an opening I could see eight or ten wood storks perched in a small cypress along the creek's edge, some with their wings half open to catch the sun's rays. Probably young of the

The inconspicuous and often overlooked water spider orchid blends in with other freshwater emergent plants in marshes, ditches and canals. *Pete Laurie.*

year, like the Copper's hawk, these birds had hatched nearby just months ago and had spent the summer learning to fend for themselves. I turned east through Catholic Hill and then toward Ritter, pausing at a freshwater wetland just before the road crossed the upper Ashepoo River. A little group of wood storks and white ibises flushed from the shallow water interspersed with old cypress stumps. Mosquito fern, brick red in the sun, carpeted much of the open water, where bream, probably redbreast, popped at the surface. Cloudless sulphur butterflies, not yet abundant this year, probed the crimson blooms of an escaped cypress vine while bumblebees and flower flies worked the lemony flowers in a clump of evening primrose species. Hidden among the vegetation, a green anole waited for an unsuspecting pollinator. A few yards farther, where the narrow bridge crossed the river, cicadas screeched from the tops of the cypress and tupelo, but the bright prothonotary warblers that had lit up the dark swamp in May had long ago left for their tropical wintering grounds.

Summer, with its heat, humidity and biting insects, serves as the ACE Basin's least appealing season. Yet the reproduction, growth and production of summer sets the stage for the bounty of autumn.

Fall

As the long days of summer grow shorter in fall, many plants and animals, very attuned to changes in the length of daylight, begin to alter their metabolism and their behavior. Some plants suddenly sprout, others begin to bloom and then produce seed and many others slow their metabolism in preparation for winter dormancy. Among the bloomers, fall wildflowers offer as much color and variety as spring flowers, with yellow a favorite fall color. Meanwhile, summer's green of chlorophyll begins to fade from the leaves of hardwoods, letting red and yellow pigments show through. Deer go into rut, the bucks rubbing the velvet from their antlers and their necks bulging as they trail receptive does. Squirrels begin to cache acorns, and foxes, bobcats and other mammals grow thicker coats.

Birds especially seem to have an acute awareness of the diminishing photoperiod. Tropical species that have spent the spring and summer nesting in the ACE change in behavior and appearance as they prepare for the long journey south for the winter. Lacking the springtime urgency to reach breeding areas, birds in fall drift south more casually, driven by the instinctive knowledge that local food supplies will soon diminish. Many birds molt in early fall, the males often taking on a drabber plumage, their singing now silenced until another spring. Omnivorous species, such as painted buntings and cardinals, switch their diets away from insect larvae, now not as abundant as seeds. The aggressive, territorial nesting behavior of male songbirds suddenly so completely reverses that these same birds form large, tightly knit flocks.

By mid-September, as I walked the dike to the beach at Botany Bay, the yellow blooms of sea oxeye had turned to brown seed husks. Draping the dog fennel, pink morning glories attracted cloudless sulfur butterflies and busy ground bumblebees while a trumpet creeper vine still bloomed from its perch on a palmetto tree. In a wet spot of high marsh after an overnight full moon tide, a single least sandpiper, its yellow legs reflecting the morning sun, probed the mud. Nearby a whimbrel inserted the entire length of its long curved bill into a fiddler crab hole and emerged with the crab firmly in its grasp. After a few shakes, it quickly swallowed its prize. On the sandy dike, several young painted buntings in the light yellowish-green of fledglings searched for grit needed to digest the seeds that would make up much of their fall and winter diet. Five semi-palmated plovers flying just above the spartina zipped by calling to one another.

In the calm waters just off the beach, a shrimp trawler dragged its twin nets south to north, with another trawler a half mile behind on the same track, probably harvesting the first of the fall white shrimp crop flushed from the creeks after a week of heavy showers. Laughing gulls and royal terns perched on the rigging waiting for the deck hands to haul back the nets and dump the catch. A single common tern, perhaps on the way to its wintering grounds in Florida, flew steadily southward.

Inland from the beach, Botany Bay's fallow fields had taken on the yellow blooms of the season in thick stands of bladder pod and sickle pod, or coffee weed. Gerardia covered one field with a lavender wash as a rice rat scampered across the clods of a recently disked strip in a dove field bright with blooming sunflowers. In the open pine-oak woodlands, the white blooms of clustered bush mint and melanthera attracted gulf fritillaries, and scattered patches of American beauty berry sported whole branches of purple fruit. A small clump of spotted horsemint bloomed in a sunny corner. In wooded openings, I looked for the fruiting heads of devil's walking stick, usually an attractant for early fall migrants such as thrushes and warblers. After some searching, I finally located a veery high in a clump of muscadine vines dotted with bunches of these native grapes. Veerys, an early but unpredictable

A commercial shrimp trawler works the shallow bottom just off the beach at Botany Bay Plantation. *Pete Laurie.*

migrant—and the least spotted of the eastern thrushes—seldom stay long in the area, often passing through unnoticed by many birders. Flying at night, veerys and other migrating songbirds spend the day feeding and resting for the next night's continued push to the south.

Many fall migrants relish the berries of the black gum, or black tupelo. An unusually large black gum grows along Donnelley's Boynton Nature Trail just where it dips down into the wetlands. Black gums seem to prefer wet edges, seldom growing in standing water, as the related water tupelo does. On a September morning, the big tree at first seemed devoid of birds, but after a few minutes, I first saw a veery and then a handful of summer tanagers that came and went, followed by a group of catbirds that shuttled back and forth from an adjacent muscadine tangle. A red-eyed vireo eventually joined them. Looking almost straight up made identifying these active and completely silent birds tricky, especially since the small, black berries they sought grew hidden near the tips of the branches. The tanagers may have nested locally, but they acted like migrants and probably had recently arrived from the northern part of their range, which extends into central Ohio. Do these migrants remember individual food sources, such as this productive tree, from one year to the next the way other birds seem to remember bird feeders along their migration routes?

September finds gray squirrels feeding on the seeds of green pinecones high among the loblolly branches. Discarded pinecone scales, the seeds stripped clean by the squirrels and then dropped from above, littered the ground as I walked the Seaboard Coast Trail at the Hollings National Wildlife Refuge in mid-September. The squirrels, however, would soon turn their attention to the usually abundant oak mast, which vary in shape from the bullet-like acorns of live oaks to fat, round overcup acorns. For squirrels, the bounty of autumn brings with it the plague of "wolves," the larvae of the squirrel botfly. This large, black fly lays its eggs on twigs and leaves in early fall. Upon hatching, the larvae attach themselves to passing squirrels; enter the animal's body through the mouth, the anus or a wound; and then move to the upper torso. Here, the larvae feed on the squirrel's bodily fluids, forming a raised welt with a breathing hole at the tip. After several weeks, the larva emerges and drops to the ground, where it remains as a pupa throughout the winter and spring before emerging as an adult. These large grubs just under their skin must cause the squirrels considerable discomfort, yet most squirrels seem little affected by these parasites. I have seen healthy-looking, normal-behaving gray squirrels with as many as six wolves sprouting from their backs.

The wooded portion of the Seaboard Coast Trail soon opened up to a tall dike that crossed acres of wetlands as it approached the Edisto River. Engineers built this dike to support rail traffic, making it much higher, wider and more substantial than typical rice field dikes. As a result, mature red oaks and large, ancient-looking live oaks grew along the berm as it towered ten to twelve feet above the wetlands to either side. In early fall, smartweed, panic grass and cattails cover these impoundments, leaving no open water. This far upstream, the Edisto, while still tidal, flows completely fresh and requires a very different management scheme than that used in the brackish portions of the river.

With no salinity available, these fields do not support the growth of widgeon grass, dwarf spike rush and the other waterfowl plants that form the mainstay on properties closer to the coast, such as Bear Island. Abandoning the alternate flooding and draining of these impoundments during the spring and summer, here the refuge staff keep water off the bed throughout the growing season, employing a moist soils management technique that favors native freshwater plants. Late in the fall, after panic grass and smartweed have shed their seeds, refuge staff burn the standing vegetation and then open the trunk doors to the river, flooding the fields just as the ducks begin to arrive for the winter. With the vegetation removed, open water, held at a depth of about ten to twelve inches, allows waterfowl to pick the seeds from the bottom mud.

In mid-September, the old railroad bed stretched high and dry across these green wetlands toward the distant Edisto. Rattlebox, that common weed of disturbed soils, showed all three stages: a few still with yellow blooms; most with green, bulging seed pods; and a couple with the dry, brown seed pods that give the plant its common name. A few blazing stars had just commenced blooming along with the ubiquitous morning glories and goldenrod. Several cardinals and a male blue grosbeak hopped in and out through the mesh of a large wire hog trap, baited with shelled corn. Feral hogs, a nonnative species but long a component of the southeastern ecology, root up and consume all manner of grubs, worms, snakes and native plants, often damaging dikes in the process. Highly adaptive, omnivorous and with a rapid rate of reproduction, they become impossible to eradicate despite the constant efforts of property managers. Trapping at the refuge probably keeps the population of hogs at least somewhat in check. While coyotes and bobcats may take an occasional young pig, the adults have no natural predators and thrive in the ACE Basin's many habitats.

At the river, the railroad dike ended abruptly where a trestle once carried freight and passengers across the Edisto to points south. An ancient, spreading live oak and several large cypress trees marked the dike's terminus. To the south, a lower dike, apparently repaired not too many years ago, paralleled the river, wide and serene just fifty yards away. In the river, close to the bank,

Goldenrod blooms along the edge of the high salt marsh. *Pete Laurie.*

I could see the pole supporting the NERR water quality data recorder I had visited by boat two months earlier. Among the tracks of deer and hogs on the sandy surface of the dike, a female velvet ant searched for the scent of buried wasp larvae. A wasp itself (only the males have wings), velvet ants seldom appear until late summer or early fall. These large, attractive insects, with their fuzzy coat of brick red and black, pack a fierce sting if handled or stepped on with bare feet. Several species of predatory wasps, including cicada killers, capture and paralyze other insects or spiders and then carry or drag them to an area of loose dirt, such as a dike top. There, they stuff their immobile but still alive prey into a quickly dug hole and then lay one or more eggs in the hole and carefully cover it over. Upon hatching, the larvae then have a fresh meal of living flesh on which to feed. Velvet ants can sniff out and dig into these secret stashes to lay their own eggs, from which velvet ant larvae emerge to eat the original wasp's larvae as well as the paralyzed larder.

Retracing my steps on the railroad dike, I soon encountered a loose flock of early migrating songbirds. I first noticed a male parula warbler foraging among the leathery leaves of a live oak. Since I had not heard or seen a parula in almost two months, I guessed this bird had nested much farther north. Several palm warblers, normally birds of open field edges, flitted back and forth through the bushes and trees lining the dike. Palm warblers, some of which spend the winter locally, often appear briefly in unusual habitats during migration. After flying all night, they drop from the sky, hungry and tired, to forage wherever they happen to land. Joining them, an immature male yellow throat, with just a hint of the black mask it will develop by next spring, perched in a dead bush just ten feet away, not at all concerned by my presence.

On another fall day just across the river at Bear Island, I stopped at Mathewes Canal in the Springfield Marsh area. Six royal terns circled fifty feet or so above the water. With high-pitched cries, they dove repeatedly on small fish congregated near one of the trunks on the canal. In these freshwater habitats, I almost never see royal terns, which normally frequent front beaches. Caspian terns I would have expected, not royal terns. However, the Edisto flowed just a half mile or so away, and with the tide high, this group of royal terns, perhaps just passing by, might have noticed these bait fish schooling in the canal. In preparation for the soon-to-arrive waterfowl, ponds at Bear Island stood at duck depth to get the maximum growth from widgeon grass and dwarf spike rush. With the water that deep, wading birds had little habitat in which to feed and had become scarce. Other than a few blue-winged teal, always among the first ducks of fall, I saw only a single pied-billed grebe and a few of the resident mottled ducks. Along the dikes, Elliot's aster bloomed in a couple of spots, and dense clumps of red berries bent down the winged sumac bushes.

Among fall blooming plants, few better characterize ACE Basin wetlands than sesbania, which occurs in two similar species. Up to ten feet tall, with feathery compound leaves, these legumes sprout from wet areas and disturbed soil, sometimes forming large stands. Hemp sesbania produces purple flowers and long, curved seedpods. The more common rattle bush has yellow flowers that develop into peapod-like fruit that dangle from the branched stems. When dry, the seeds become loose and rattle around in the pod, giving the plant its common name. Both sesbanias casually resemble two unrelated fall wetland edge plants: bladder pod and sickle pod. Unfortunately, none of these often abundant plants appears to have much direct benefit to wildlife.

However, many other native plants provide great benefit to a variety of wildlife species. In early fall, red-winged blackbirds seem to relish the seeds of giant cord grass. At Donnelley WMA, I came upon a flock of at least five hundred busily working the tops of this common wetland plant. The flock contained only male birds, a not uncommon occurrence among the blackbird family (female blackbirds form their own sex-specific flocks). This flocking behavior marked a dramatic change from just a couple months previous, when male redwings set up and vigorously defended nesting territories, proudly displaying their red epaulets; endlessly repeating their croaking, "Conk-a-ree" from daylight to dark; and sending stray male redwings packing with spirited pursuits. But with the breeding season over, these same males suddenly become best pals, packing together in tight, restless flocks, their low chirps and creaks keeping the flock together, a complete behavioral reversal analogous to diurnal songbirds suddenly becoming nocturnal migrants in the fall.

Another fall icon, orb-weaving spiders, suddenly appeared throughout ACE Basin woodlands beginning in late August. One autumn day, I watched a crab-backed spider spin a huge web, working methodically from outside to inside, moving counterclockwise. The spider stretched each silk strand a quarter inch apart from the previous one, on schedule to have the web completed by dusk, when it probably became most effective for entangling moths and other night fliers. Better-known and more abundant, the much larger golden silk spider sometimes constructs a web thirty feet or higher from tree to tree, but many stay closer to the ground, where they wait patiently for flying prey to become entangled. Seen in the sunlight from just the right angle, the silken web has a golden hue that perhaps makes the strands less visible to flying insects. Orb weaving represents one of the most complex tasks accomplished by any invertebrate, a fact that provides little solace to the deer hunter who, in his pre-dawn trek to a stand, suddenly gets a face full of spider web. Despite their size, golden silk spiders seldom bite, and such bites usually produce only short-lived mild reactions.

For most birds of the ACE Basin, nesting has ended by September. But at an old rice field reserve late in the month, a black-bellied whistling duck marshaled a brood of recently hatched ducklings. This odd duck, having expanded its range far to the east within the past twenty years, has a prolonged nesting season, quite unlike the area's other two nesting waterfowl species: the wood duck and the mottled duck. The six whistling duck youngsters—strikingly marked with broad brownish stripes and blue, not red, bills—already displayed the distinctive long neck of the tree duck family. On spotting me, the ducklings immediately hid behind the adult, one craning that long neck for a look over the adult's back. The hen (I assumed) soon swam off through the frog's-bit, with youngsters following obediently. This new addition to the ACE avifauna has a long breeding season that extends into the fall, in part to avoid competition for nesting cavities with the more aggressive wood duck.

In September, I had a chance to visit the ACE Basin's wood duck stronghold, the Salkehatchie Swamp. Just above the town of Yemasee, the Combahee River becomes known as the Salkehatchie River, which farther upstream divides into the Big Salkehatchie and the Little Salkehatchie. Most residents agree that the river's name changes from Combahee to Salkehatchie at the farthest reach of the tide, a point which may have moved slightly upstream in the last century or so with rising sea levels. The ACE Basin Task Force drew the project area's core boundaries to encompass this narrow neck of the Salkehatchie flood plain between Highway 21 on the east, Highway 63 on the north and Highway 13 on the west. Much of the core area's fifty-five thousand acres of forested wetlands occur in this Salkehatchie Swamp area. All of this land remains privately owned with little public access, except by boat.

For generations, Ross Catterton's family has owned property on the east side of the Salkehatchie, and he took me to see his river place on the last day of the month. About two hundred yards inside the gate off Highway 21, the entrance road drops about twenty feet down into the wide flood plain. Another quarter mile or so past a recent clear-cut on one side and hardwoods on the other, the road drops again, this time perhaps just ten or fifteen feet, into where the river floods virtually every winter. On that day, however, despite weeks of above-normal rain, the Salkehatchie stayed within its banks, flowing smoothly seaward, its water muddied by logging farther upstream.

Here, well inland, the tides do not impact the river, and this area never had any value for rice growing. Loggers, however, long ago harvested the original forest, which probably consisted of mostly cypress and water tupelo. A few medium-sized second-growth cypresses grew close to the river, along

_No —

with one huge tree the loggers somehow missed. While still green and vibrant, many of the cypress trees had produced scaly, almost spherical cones hanging from the branches. Across the river, here just forty or fifty feet wide, black willows crowded the bank, some leaning far out, their lower branches dragging in the current. A small black walnut, its roots undercut by the eroding riverbank but bearing a number of big yellow nuts, sagged horizontally across the dark water.

A small flycatcher sat alertly on the horizontal walnut trunk. Then, spotting a passing insect, the flycatcher vanished into the willows without ever revealing its identity. Three species of small flycatchers pass through the South Carolina coast on their way south each fall. All three appear almost identical to the locally nesting Acadian flycatcher. Outside their nesting habitat and usually silent, they defy identification to species unless they call since the four have quite different notes. Unfortunately, they seldom make a sound.

Ross and I walked easily among the towering swamp chestnut oaks, willow oaks and water oaks, the damp flood plain devoid of understory save for a few scattered dwarf palmettos. We kept an eye out for snakes—Ross thought us more likely to encounter a copperhead than a cottonmouth. During the often rainy winter, the river leaves its banks and floods the surrounding forest, keeping most undergrowth in check. A winding slough, its bed four or five feet below the flood plain and holding water throughout the year, finally blocked our passage. Here, a huge loblolly pine, towering into the canopy, had managed to survive for many decades among the hardwoods.

The slow-flowing Salkehatchie meanders back and forth across the flood plain, easily eroding the sandy substrate, undercutting the bank on one side while adding material on the other in a never-ending process. A short ways downriver, an eight-foot gator basked in the sun on an accreted sandbar that Ross kept mowed. Beyond the cypress trees along the river came the cry of a red-tailed hawk and the rattle of a pileated woodpecker. Interspersed among the cypress and the more dominant oaks, a few large spruce pines grew. Loggers usually avoid this uncommon species, as the soft wood has little value. As we stood on a little rough wooden dock that hung over the river's edge, an immature little blue heron, its wings fixed in a smooth, soundless glide, swept past us just a foot or two above the water to perch abruptly on a low limb fifty yards downstream. It sat there quietly for a few minutes, preening its pure white feathers in the noon sun before gliding around the next bend and out of sight. Little blue herons keep the white plumage of

A light mist covers the Salkehatchie River as it meanders past towering swamp tupelos. *Phillip Jones.*

youth throughout the fall and winter, gradually molting into the adult blue after a transition period of mottled plumage.

The forested wetlands of Salkehatchie Swamp add another dimension to the ACE Basin's diverse habitats. Although logged at different times over the years, most of this area, which includes thousands of acres along the Big Salkehatchie and the Little Salkehatchie, remains unaltered by human activity, as the swamp has little access except by foot or small boat.

In early October, as I watched a buckeye alight on a stalk of spartina at the boat ramp at Fields Point, not a typical habitat for this migrating butterfly, I realized I had seen very few butterflies of any species all fall. Late summer and early autumn often come alive with buckeyes, cloudless sulfurs and gulf fritillaries, but by October, I had seen very few. Even the normally common long-tailed skipper seemed scarce. Many factors control butterfly populations, including harsh winters, which can kill overwintering individuals, and variations in spring and early summer rainfall and temperature, which can delay or reduce the growth of larval food plants. These subtle fluctuations go unnoticed until the fall butterfly population dips well below normal. Some years, cloudless sulfurs fill the September air with their yellow dance, sometimes moving steadily north following the coastline. Meanwhile, orange and silver gulf fritillaries tap the nectar of lantana and seek out passionflower vines, a favorite food plant for their larvae. Most years, a steady stream of monarchs, those long-distance migrants, pass through sedately, sometimes pausing to feed at Joe Pye weed and other fall bloomers but mostly moving resolutely toward their Mexican winter ground. I had seen but a few monarchs, which have suffered population decline across the continent due to the overuse of herbicides that have devastated their larval plant, milkweed. By October, I also had yet to see a zebra butterfly, a regular late summer visitor that wanders up the coast from Florida. The previous two seasons, I had seen zebras daily in a variety of habitats by late July, and they had remained in the area until Christmas. Graceful, slow-flying and strikingly marked butterflies, zebras, like gulf fritillaries, seek out passionflower but often seem to just drift aimlessly through the trees, usually at eye level, making them among the easiest butterflies to identify.

The full moon tides of early fall signal the start of marsh hen hunting for those few hunters who still practice this traditional sport. Marsh hens, also called clapper rails, find abundant habitat in the ACE Basin's ninety-one thousand acres of tidal marsh, preferring salt and brackish marshes over freshwater marshes. While several species of mammals—notably raccoons, mink and otter—regularly enter the marsh to feed, no mammal actually lives in the marsh since mammals require a dry den in which to bear their young. The marsh hen, which in many ways behaves more like a mammal than a bird, spends its entire life in the marsh, filling a niche left vacant by mammals. Behaving like many mammals, marsh hens stay out of sight during the day, become more active at night and, for the most part, remain flightless. Actually, marsh hens fly quite well but seldom find the need to do so, preferring instead to skulk among the dense marsh grass, locating food and avoiding predators without taking to the air. In the spring, marsh hens weave together stalks of spartina to construct nests above the reach of the normal high tide. Should an exceptionally high tide destroy the nest, marsh hens simply rebuild and lay another clutch of eggs. The ACE Basin's considerable population of resident marsh hens gets a boost each fall with an influx of migrant birds from as far north as Connecticut. Their "clapping" calls ring from the marshes, with any sudden loud noise such as a gunshot setting off a wave of sound as bird after bird takes up the call.

The marsh hen's reluctance to fly or swim makes it an easy target for gunners, who pole small boats along the marsh edges during spring tides when the birds congregate on floating rafts of dead grass. Here, they often

Above: St. Helena Sound and the lower reaches of the ACE Basin's three rivers provide excellent habitat for blue crabs. *Phillip Jones.*

Left: Protecting wetlands through conservation easements on private lands became one of the main goals of the ACE Basin Project. *Phillip Jones.*

ACE Basin fox squirrels, highly variable in color, usually have dark-gray or black coats and often white ears and feet. *Phillip Jones.*

Sunset on the Ashepoo River. *Phillip Jones.*

Right: Immature common gallinules do not gain the black adult plumage with the red beak shield until their second spring. *Phillip Jones.*

Below: River otters occur throughout the ACE Basin's extensive wetlands from salt marshes to freshwater swamps. *Phillip Jones.*

Left: Wild azaleas bloom in early April, preferring wet woods and sunny, open pinelands. *Pete Laurie.*

Below: The nonvenomous banded water snake occurs throughout the South Carolina coastal plain, where it feeds on fish and amphibians. *Phillip Jones.*

Black-bellied whistling ducks have an extended breeding season that lasts into October. *Pete Laurie.*

Native golden canna lilies, uncommon to rare in the ACE Basin, grow in isolated wet areas, usually in thick stands. *Pete Laurie.*

Semi-palmated plovers and dunlins in flight over the dunes of Otter Island. *Phillip Jones.*

The carefully managed impoundments of the ACE Basin provide food plants that attract and hold waterfowl by the thousands throughout the winter. *Phillip Jones.*

A male wood duck, a common permanent resident of the ACE, shows off its colorful plumage. *Phillip Jones.*

Great egrets and other wading birds rear their young in numerous ACE Basin rookeries. *Phillip Jones.*

Screech owls—which have two color phases, red and gray—sometimes roost and even nest in wood duck boxes. *Phillip Jones.*

Turkey poults leave the nest within hours of hatching. *Phillip Jones.*

Duck hunters sometimes shoot hooded merganser drakes, which have little food value but make decorative wall mounts. *Phillip Jones.*

The bright plumage of male shovelers makes them easy to identify from a distance. *Phillip Jones.*

Above: Male turkeys begin to strut and gobble in March and early April in the ACE Basin. *Phillip Jones.*

Left: Golden silk spiders hang in the middle of the large webs they weave between tree branches. *Pete Laurie.*

Right: Coral bean, a common native wildflower, blooms in May along logging roads and other disturbed areas. *Pete Laurie.*

Below: Roseate spoonbills, once a rarity in the ACE Basin, have become much more numerous in recent years. *Pete Laurie.*

Left: Horsemint blooms in the early fall in sunny waste places with sandy soil. *Pete Laurie.*

Below: Early spring nesters, ospreys build huge stick nests in dead trees and on man-made structures throughout the ACE Basin. *Phillip Jones.*

Eastern box turtles roam the ACE Basin uplands, feeding on a wide variety of plants and animals. *Phillip Jones.*

A pileated woodpecker checks an old fence post for wood-boring insects. *Phillip Jones.*

Left: Hooded pitcher plants secrete a strong odor to lure the flies and other insects they consume. *Pete Laurie.*

Below: In the past twenty-five years, armadillos have gradually moved north into the ACE Basin and have now become common residents. *Phillip Jones.*

Above: Deer season in the ACE Basin begins in mid-August before many bucks have shed the velvet from their antlers. *Phillip Jones.*

Right: Male painted buntings, among the most colorful of North American birds, establish breeding territories in brushy edges throughout the ACE Basin. *Phillip Jones.*

Above: Sunny spring days bring alligators out of the water to bask on the dikes. *Pete Laurie.*

Left: The complex blossoms of horse sugar, an early spring bloomer, often develop before the new leaves open. *Pete Laurie.*

hold their ground until approached closely and then, at the last minute, take to the air somewhat feebly. On a good tide, most hunters can take their daily limit of fifteen in a short time. Marsh hens have a gamey flavor relished by many longtime coastal residents.

Marsh hen hunters occasionally encounter an otherwise seldom-seen creature riding out a big tide on a raft of dead spartina stalks. Mink regularly prowl salt marshes but in small numbers, active mostly at night. At high tide, mink climb aboard rafts of vegetation often far from high ground, in part to avoid the larger land predators, such as raccoons and bobcats. Secure on these rafts, they may pause to devour a blue crab or even to nurse young. More abundant in the Piedmont than on the coast and scarce in marshes north of Charleston, these fierce little weasels have a varied diet, eating whatever they find available. In the salt marsh, they consume crabs of various kinds, along with small fishes, rice rats and rails, including marsh hens. Although trappers take some mink (more in the Piedmont than on the coast), biologists attribute today's much-reduced mink population to pollutants. In one study, more than 40 percent of trapped mink showed levels of mercury and PCBs high enough to possibly interfere with reproduction.

One early October morning, I recorded the fall's first three common wintering raptors, the vanguard of the migration. First, a kestrel dove from a power line, its sickle-shaped wings carrying it across a field of corn stubble. Then about noon that day, I saw the season's first harrier winging easily above the impoundments at Bear Island. Harriers find the ACE Basin's extensive wetlands ideal hunting grounds for small birds and rodents that constitute most of their diet. Females always outnumber males locally, as most male harriers spend the winter farther north and inland. Later, a slim shape on a dead branch at the top of a distant pecan caught my eye. My binoculars revealed an adult sharp-shinned hawk, that terror of small songbirds, preening its wings and barred tail. The diminutive size suggested a male as opposed to the noticeably larger female sharp-shin. Sharp-shins have modified their migration pattern in the eastern continent considerably in the last forty years. Once, these raptors, most of which nest far to the north, passed along the South Carolina coast in great numbers each autumn, with many staying to spend the winter. Today, however, much of the population remains in New England and Upstate New York, apparently finding plenty of the small birds that constitute most of the sharp-shins' prey. Global warming and the proliferation of bird feeders, which concentrate small birds, both might have played a role in changing the sharp-shin's migration pattern.

Another common migrant, the phoebe, also arrives for the winter in early October, some years appearing almost everywhere across the ACE. I watched a recently arrived phoebe struggle with a large dragonfly it had caught, shaking and manipulating this awkward meal until it suddenly swallowed the thing whole. Of the area's two migrant woodpeckers, flickers (a few of which nest locally most years) usually arrive first, but a yellow-bellied sapsucker surprised me in early October, a good month ahead of schedule. Autumn birdlife also includes many transients just passing through. Redstarts have a prolonged migratory season, often arriving by early August, with a few stragglers still wandering through during November. However, most of these fall redstarts wear the more subdued fawn and yellow plumage of the females and immatures. I rarely see an adult male with its fiery orange and black fluttering among the autumn treetops. Catbirds also pass through each fall in considerable numbers. Bushy hedgerows and edges sometimes seem full of the cautious gray birds with long tails, and you can often hear their distinctive "mew" from deep within the underbrush. As with many fall migrants, a few catbirds will spend the winter in the ACE while the majority continues south to the Gulf Coast. They only rarely nest on the South Carolina coast.

With migrants dominating the bird life, I sometimes forget about the equally interesting resident birds. Walking past one of the many plastic nest boxes put up for barn owls at Bear Island, I flushed one of these rare owls. Appearing completely white from the underside, it flew across an open area and into a thick stand of live oaks draped with Spanish moss. This most secretive and silent of the local owls seldom appears during daylight hours. A scientific supply company donated barn owl nest boxes (which DNR staff placed on tall poles across the mostly treeless expanse of Bear Island) in exchange for owl pellets, which the company collects to sell to schools. Owls swallow small mammals whole, digest the parts they can and then regurgitate the bones, teeth and hair in compact pellets. A close examination of the pellets provides insights to the birds' diet, making owl pellets much in demand for biology classes. The owls benefit from the donated boxes by having many more places to nest and roost, and Bear Island gets increased control of rice rats, cotton rats and other small rodents.

Every fall day seems to bring another wildflower. The yellow flowers of southern crown head suddenly brighten a damp shaded spot while its white-blooming relative, tickweed, takes over whole acres of the pine-oak woods at Botany Bay. Evergreen goldenrod borders the wetland edges, and the dainty blooms of salt marsh aster line fields of spartina and needle rush. Lavender

Big-eared bats spend the day clinging to the ceiling of an abandoned house in the ACE Basin. *Phillip Jones.*

spikes of blazing star light up the understory in the pine flat woods and other disturbed places, the lighter-colored variety usually more prevalent, although the smaller, darker purple blooms erupt here and there. In planted fields, volunteer morning glories produce a profusion of purple blooms, their trailing vines dragging down the brown stalks of corn, sunflowers and small grains that earlier brought in doves for September shoots.

Octobers with good weather hold a few summer birds that linger after most of their kind have headed south. On a nice morning at Botany Bay, I saw a single female painted bunting when the majority of that ubiquitous summer species had already made its way south to Cuba and the Bahamas. At the far end of Jason's Lake, I counted six roseate spoonbills, bright pink in the sunlit top of a live oak. Once a very rare late summer visitor to South Carolina, these colorful waders now arrive every summer in considerable numbers and stay well into the fall. Glancing across Botany Bay's extensive salt marsh, the spartina topped with golden seeds, I noticed a large dark bird at the top of a dead pine. Through binoculars, I recorded the first bald eagle of the year, this one in the dark plumage of a juvenile. Minutes later, a full-plumaged adult, white head and tail gleaming, flew across the marsh to settle into another dead pine a few hundred yards away. Having spent

Uncommon in the ACE Basin, southern crownsbeard prefers damp, shaded hardwoods. *Pete Laurie.*

Tickseed, a tall perennial, blooms in the fall in wooded areas all across the ACE Basin. *Pete Laurie.*

the summer at Chesapeake Bay, the Great Lakes region or other northern areas, eagles begin to drift back to the ACE Basin in the fall to set up territories and get ready for December nesting.

Like much of the ACE Basin, South Fenwick Island has a long agricultural past but now has reverted back to something closer to its natural state. Once just the southern tip of Fenwick Island, South Fenwick became a separate island in 1904, when the Intracoastal Waterway cut it off from access by anything but boat. For decades afterward, inhabitants of the five-hundred-acre island grew cotton, vegetables and other crops. Ten to fifteen families farmed the island, fishing and crabbing in the adjacent waters where the Edisto and Ashepoo Rivers pinch together just before entering St. Helena Sound. Isolation eventually proved too great an obstacle, and the last permanent residents moved to the mainland in the late 1970s.

I rode over to South Fenwick on a clear October morning in a small outboard with Dewey Wise, who bought most of the island in

The common blazing star of the ACE Basin, which often occurs in scattered clumps, blooms in early fall in sandy pinewoods. *Pete Laurie.*

the 1980s. Wise lives in a spacious modern home that he built on North Fenwick a few years ago. The boat ride from the dock at his house to the dock at his tractor shed on South Fenwick took less than ten minutes. Other than the tractor shed and a small church, the island has no other structures, although the foundations of a couple of the larger ancient dwellings still lurk among the undergrowth. In an old pickup truck, Wise drove around the island, stopping often to point out various changes he has seen and recent modifications, including five small ponds he dug in low wet spots and now keeps filled with rainwater.

Aerial photographs from the 1940s and 1950s show South Fenwick as completely open fields with a few wooded spots and a fringe of bushes and trees. Since farming ended seventy years ago, groves of oaks have grown up, and maritime forests of live oak, loblolly pine, cabbage palmetto, red cedar and yaupon holly have developed on parts of both the north and south ends. Wise planted a few pines and bald cypress trees, but much of the sandy soil remains covered with native herbaceous plants, especially bluestem grass. The owner just before Wise planted soybeans one year, but deer ate most of that crop. Wise himself had the same problem the one year he planted corn. Hunters now take ten to fifteen deer per year on the island; the deer population annually increases through reproduction and from additions that swim across the two-hundred-yard-wide Intracoastal Waterway. During the heyday of farming, island residents probably harvested every deer they saw, keeping the population very low.

Despite the now abundant oaks, the gray squirrels seem scarce, and Wise said he had never seen a fox squirrel on the island. Unlike deer, squirrels do not swim well and probably rarely attempt to cross the Cut, as locals refer to the dredged waterway. During the long reign of agriculture on the island, squirrels would have enjoyed little habitat. They also probably sustained considerable hunting pressure by the subsistence farmers, perhaps to the point of extirpation. Nor have armadillos made it to the island, at least not yet, although Wise did see a coyote on South Fenwick. He also has seen a number of eastern diamond-backed rattlesnakes but no canebrake rattlers, copperheads or cottonmouths. Better yet, we saw no evidence of hogs on the island, although residents over many generations almost certainly raised hogs for food.

On the island's eastern side, a dike built decades ago by previous owners once cut off a small creek and an adjoining finger of salt marsh that extended inland from Fish Creek. The dike had breached long before Wise bought the property, and rather than repair the dike, he built a wooden bridge across the break. The former impoundment has now reverted back to naturally functioning marsh. The entire island serves as an example of the effects of human manipulation of the environment and how, over time, nature can reclaim such areas although not always to an exact replica of the original. Near the middle of the island, we spotted another relic of human disturbance: a cow skull, bleached white, with one horn still attached.

"I know exactly what animal this came from," Wise said with a smile, picking it up and placing it in the back of the truck. Not long after purchasing this land, Wise brought in a few head of beef cattle, which in just a few years grew to a herd of about forty. He decided that many cows would soon damage the natural environment, so he rounded them up, barged them to the mainland and sold the whole lot. One young bull, however, escaped the roundup and, for many more years, lived a solitary life on the island, where Wise rarely saw him. Wise knew the bull eventually died, but now he had proof.

A much more natural part of the environment, mistletoe, sprouted from the tops of several oaks on the south end of the island but, in October, remained weeks away from developing its decorative white berries. In South Fenwick's fallow fields, large, grayish grasshoppers got up and flew weakly across the tops of the bluestem. Two meadowlarks flushed ahead of the truck as we followed one of the little-used dirt tracks. Not a locally breeding bird but common in open areas throughout the ACE during the winter, meadowlarks usually travel in loose flocks of fifteen to fifty birds. Birdwatchers commonly see them in flight, their shallow wing beats interspersed with long glides, from mid-fall into early spring. Back at the tractor shed after our brief tour of this unique part of the ACE, I noted a dozen or more cast-off exoskeletons of cicadas clinging to the building's siding, just where the emergent grubs had abandoned them to start the short-lived, aboveground adult portion of their lives. South Fenwick reflects the history of much of the ACE Basin: the original habitat altered and intensively farmed for centuries sits now mostly unpopulated, undeveloped and reverting back to a more natural state.

A few mornings later, I joined Nick Wallover, manager of the ACE Basin NERR, on his monthly shorebird survey on the beaches of Otter and Pine Islands. Wallover selects a day during the month with a morning high tide to conduct his survey, and I wanted to see how shorebird populations had changed since my last trip with him in late July. With the tide covering the hundreds of acres of salt marsh mud flat, shorebirds of a variety of species move to the narrow sandy beaches of Otter and Pine, where they stand patiently waiting for the falling tide to re-expose their foraging areas. The short boat ride from Bennetts Point to the north end of Otter left our ears stinging in the chilly October air, but once we reached the narrow strip of sand left by the tide, the rising sun over a calm Atlantic made for pleasant birding. Through a spotting scope, Wallover started counting the bunched flocks of willets, dowitchers and semi-palmated plovers with their neat brown neckbands. He noted small groups of sanderlings, a few least sandpipers and even a couple late red knots. Except for the sanderlings, a few of which chased the retreating waves to pluck small invertebrates from the wet sand, none of these birds normally forage on the beach, using it strictly to loaf and wait out the high tide. At any time other than high tide, they disperse across the estuary and become difficult to accurately census.

Numerous fresh otter tracks ran the length of the high tide beach, here just a narrow wind-swept strip between the murmuring surf and salt marsh. The short-legged otters with their hunched gait leave neat rows of two paw prints side by side, quite distinct from raccoon tracks. A flock of a dozen common grackles roamed the shallow dunes, where small clumps of sea oats bent over, heavy with seeds. We soon covered this short length of beach and, re-boarding the boat, eased across the front of adjacent Pine Island, on this calm morning an easy trip to the mouth of the Edisto, and then upriver a short ways to land on the inlet beach of Pine. Not really a front beach, this accreting strip of sand greatly exceeded the beach of Otter Island, which had experienced considerable erosion in recent years.

Between the Pine Island beach and the marsh behind, I flushed a pale-colored raccoon that bounded away through the salt hay and sea ox-eye. In bare spots, salicornia had just begun to turn from green to red. As we walked along the sand, protected here from the direct surf, Wallover stopped occasionally to set up his spotting scope and counted several large flocks of shorebirds. Species composition differed little from what we had just recorded on Otter, but with more beach, we noted greater numbers, including a late season marbled godwit, a likewise lingering Wilson's plover and several piping plovers, paler and with shorter bills than the more numerous semi-palmated plovers. As on Otter, all sat motionless, staring into the breeze, many on just one leg, the other tucked out of sight in their breast feathers. Our total count of shorebirds on the two island beaches that morning exceeded 2,300 birds of fourteen species. Dowitchers made up more than half of that total, with the brightly marked semi-palmated plovers constituting another quarter. Both of these species commonly winter along the South Carolina coast.

Whether the birds waiting out high tide that day represented a large portion of the shorebirds present in the St. Helena Sound area or just a small sample, we had no way of knowing since other scattered high spots also provide a refuge for marsh shorebirds during high tides. However, over a period of years, this monthly survey will show changes in population levels, range shifts and seasonal variations. Combined with the many similar surveys all along the eastern seaboard, these data help researchers track changes in the numbers and movements of shorebirds, often indicators of environmental issues.

THE SEASONS

As the tide slipped away from the beach, it exposed a strip of spartina stumps that the high tide had earlier submerged. The shifting sand had months ago overwashed the marsh, but the dense roots still held the dead stalks in place. At one spot on the intertidal sand, green splotches of sea lettuce, pulled loose by the currents, decorated the wet sand. Among the sea lettuce lay a single transparent jellyfish. Wallover picked it up carefully by the bell and identified it as a four-sided boxjelly, also called a sea wasp, an unpleasant stinging species at times common along the South Carolina coast. Crossing a sliver of salt marsh just behind the sandy inlet, we flushed a dark sparrow. After just a quick flight, it dropped back into the thick grass. In short order, we flushed several more of these seaside sparrows just returning to their wintering habitat. A very habitat-specific species, seaside sparrows nest along the edges of brackish and freshwater marshes, sometimes well inland. In the fall, however, they move to salt marshes where they stay out of sight among the spartina stalks, almost never venturing onto the surrounding highland.

While many birds gather into large flocks in the fall, one local bird certainly does not form flocks during the winter. Individual mockingbirds stake out and fiercely defend winter feeding territory, centered on a source of berries. Preferred berries include holly, palmetto, red cedar, poison ivy, pyracantha and privet. Birds that join large nomadic winter flocks gamble that they can locate multiple sources of food as they roam across large ranges. Mockingbirds, on the other hand, bet on a sure thing, and once they stake out a food source, they seldom leave it until spring. While they seem to ignore most other bird species, they instantly spot and attack any potential berry eater, including robins, hermit thrushes, catbirds and, of course, other mockingbirds. Should a passing flock of voracious cedar waxwings descend on a mockingbird's larder, the overwhelmed mocker goes into a frenzy of often futile attacks on the many invaders.

I watched a mockingbird in late November at Bennetts Point briefly attack an outside mirror of a parked car, even though the car had arrived at that spot just minutes earlier and half a dozen people stood within forty feet of the car. In just those few minutes, the ever-alert mockingbird had caught a glimpse of its reflection in the mirror and thought a rival mocker had invaded its feeding territory. The mockingbird's so completely opposite behavior from most winter birds seems to serve it well, although one wonders just how a mockingbird can inventory a very local supply of berries and assess the chances of not running out of food before spring. The omnivorous mocker, of course, supplements its diet of berries with insects and insect larvae whenever possible.

THE ACE BASIN

Wetlands throughout the ACE Basin attract a variety of rails, among the most secretive of birds. Some rails such as clapper and king live in the ACE year-round as permanent residents. Others move into the area from the north each fall. Freshwater wetlands that have grown up in native grasses and other plants provide excellent habitat for most rails. In the fall, managers of these wetlands commonly mow and then burn freshwater impoundments prior to flooding them for wintering waterfowl. This practice provides open water while removing the summer plant growth, leaving just the seeds and roots of panic grass and red root, both ideal duck food. The mowing and burning operations flush the secretive rails from their dense grass habitats into the sparser vegetation along the edges of the fields.

One November some years ago, the staff at Bear Island WMA told me about all the small rails they had seen the day before while mowing a large impoundment near the Edisto River. The soil in most of this freshwater wetland will support tractors when completely drained, although the remnants of old cypress stumps hidden in the thick stands of panic grass and red root make mowing a challenge. Hoping to get a good look at these rails, I spent an hour or so driving an ATV through the waist-deep vegetation covering eight or ten acres that the bush hogs had spared for the moment. I flushed about twenty American bitterns, a secretive wading bird that I did not expect to see at that density. Better yet, I also flushed several tiny black rails, the smallest and most elusive of all North American rails. Like many of their kind, black rails rarely take wing, preferring to run ahead of an intruder, always out of sight in the grass. You cannot walk them up, nor can most bird dogs flush them. The noise of a tractor or ATV moving at a good pace panics them into short flights of just a second or two above the tops of the grass stalks. Their size and dark plumage with white specks would identify them, provided my glance caught those cues in the quick flight. Flushed once, no amount of crisscrossing the same area would put the same bird up again. I repeated this same performance a few days later, recording in those two days six or seven black rails, the only ones I had ever seen.

Hoping to duplicate that success, I joined DNR biologist Christy Hand on the last day of October as we drove a similar ATV into the same five-hundred-acre field and followed a big tractor as the operator, Bear Island staffer Cathy Cook, mowed down the year's crop of panic grass and red root. The previous day, Hand had ridden in the cab of the tractor with Cook as she mowed an eleven-acre adjacent field. Hand had counted an amazing 182 sora rails in less than five hours. Larger than black rails, and much more common and less secretive, sora rails breed much farther north, passing along the South Carolina coast on their way south in the fall, with quite a few spending the winter locally. Still, that many in such a small area seemed excessive and further emphasized the value of impoundments to so many birds other than waterfowl.

Hand, however, had not seen a black rail, so we drove the ATV slowly parallel to the tractor hoping one of the elusive little birds would jump from the grass. After a couple hours, we had seen about ten soras, which flew up just ahead of the tractor's front wheels, crossed the mowed stubble and dove into the unmowed edge grasses. Hand tried to photograph each as it passed in front of us or circled back into the still standing vegetation. Two birds that offered a slightly longer look appeared lighter colored, but we dismissed those as immature soras. To our disappointment, we did not see a black rail. However, that evening, as Hand checked her photographs—most just of blurs—a very sharp image of a light-colored bird as it paused for a second on the mowed grass drew her attention. She immediately e-mailed the photograph to an expert on yellow rails who confirmed her identification of this other very secretive, rarely seen little rail. I had expected to see soras and had hoped to see black rails, but I had not thought much about yellow rails, a species I had never before seen. However, Hand's great photograph clearly showed the dark line through the eye and the distinctly striped back. In a second photograph of the bird in flight, the white wing patches stood out. The size difference, just an inch or so smaller than a sora, we had not noticed during the brief view we had of the bird. So now, nine years apart, I had recorded two of the most difficult birds to see in all of North America, both in the same field.

Later that week, I got a chance to perch on the jump seat in the cab of the big tractor, that day operated by Matt Smoak, one of the other technicians at Bear Island. The comfortable cab muffled the engine's roar and the whir of the bush hog blades, leaving only the snap and crackle of sesbania stems slapping the tractor's undercarriage. Countless song sparrows and swamp sparrows moved through the tall vegetation, staying just ahead of us, and several species of small rails jumped up and flew in short arcs just above the grass before diving again for cover. In two hours I counted fifty-four sora rails, about twenty-five Virginia rails and four yellow rails, one of which scurried from in front of the tractor and hid in the swath we had just mowed. Matt stopped the tractor, and I jumped off and approached within a few feet of the hidden rail. It darted from its hiding place, ran a yard or two and then flapped feebly to the edge of the nearby canal. At such close range, I could distinctly see the yellow striping with black bars across the back and the white wing patches when it flew.

A rarely seen yellow rail tries to hide in a just mowed field at Bear Island WMA.
Christy Hand.

All three of these seemingly weakly flying rail species nest much farther north but somehow manage to migrate to the South Carolina coast and farther south each fall. Hunters, birdwatchers and others who spend a lot of time in these habitats during the fall and winter see Virginia rails and sora rails on occasion, but the much more secretive yellow rail rarely shows itself. Without the noise and disturbance of the tractor as it leveled the vegetation, we would never have seen any yellow rails, yet they obviously inhabit these wetlands in considerable numbers. Soras and yellow rails eat small snails and insects, as well as weed seeds. Virginia rails use their longer bills to probe the mud for a variety of mollusks to supplement smartweed seeds and even duckweed. We flushed most of the Virginia rails on the first pass around the canal that bordered the field. As the mower moved farther toward the field's center, I saw fewer Virginias and more soras in addition to the four yellow rails. Our total rail count, covering seven separate days from late October to early December, came to 281 soras, 33 Virginia rails and 36 yellow rails. Although Christy and I had recorded what seemed like a great number of rails, those numbers probably represented only a small portion of rails present across the hundreds of acres of this prime habitat.

A few days after flushing the rails, I rode in an ATV with manager Ross Catterton as he burned one of the freshwater impoundments that staff had

A fire tornado erupts with a roar when fires set on the edges of a large field at Bear Island WMA burn together. *Pete Laurie.*

mowed a week earlier. We started in the southeast corner, the wind mostly westward. Earlier in the day, Smoak had used a tiller to cut a wide fire line all around the field and around each of the several islands of vegetation that held a duck blind. The border of fresh dirt confined the fire, keeping it safely within the mowed area. Ross sped along the edges of the fire lines, holding a drip torch over the dry grass and stubble. Little fires leapt up with every flaming drop of kerosene. The fire flushed an occasional sparrow and grasshopper, but no rails emerged from the flat expanse of mowed grass and stubble.

Matt soon joined us on a four-wheeler, lighting more fire lines with another drip torch. In thirty minutes we had fires started along all the edges and around each of the several duck blinds. The variable wind drove the fire this way and that across the dry grass, the orange flames crackling and snapping as they turned to white and then gray smoke that rose like a curtain across the sunny sky. Gradually, the fires on each edge moved toward the middle of the field. We stopped the vehicles to watch as it all came together with the roar of a fire tornado that erupted into a thin, dark funnel cloud that snaked and danced its way upward through the dense gray smoke. And then silence came as the fire collapsed, all fuel exhausted, leaving a blackened landscape with nothing left but the tiny seeds of panic grass and the succulent red roots just below the surface. We had burned the entire 175 acres in just under an hour. We drove out of the impoundment and directly to the trunk that connected the field to its water source at Mathewes Canal. Ross and Matt raised the outside door of the trunk a few inches, and water surged through, pushed open the inside door and rushed into the canal surrounding the now blackened field. Ross said that within a day, water would cover the entire bed and provide open water and food throughout the winter for pintails, gadwall, widgeon and other waterfowl.

Left unmowed and unburned, these fields would grow up in cattails, woody plants and other species of little value to wildlife in just a few years. While the rails and sparrows lose habitat for the short term and must disperse to edges and more marginal habitat, they gain it right back the following spring once managers drain the water and allow preferred species, such as panic grass and red root, to return. The mowing operation itself flushes most of the rails unharmed. However, old stumps in parts of these fields limit bush hogging and require burning part of the crop as standing grasses. This may result in some mortality of these small, secretive rails so reluctant to fly. However, a couple of weeks later, Christy and I rode in the ATV as Ross and Matt burned the five-hundred-acre field where much of the grass remained unmowed. We thought the fire moving quickly and loudly with lots of flame and smoke would flush out more rails, but we saw just one sora. Immediately after the fire had burned itself out, leaving just blackened stubble and a few wisps of smoke, Christy and I walked through a couple parts of the field. Finding no little piles of charred feathers, we concluded any remaining rails

This LeConte's sparrow found little cover when it returned to a burned-over field just minutes after the fire swept through. *Christy Hand.*

had escaped the fire. We did flush a single sora that had hidden under a stump either to escape the fire or to seek the little bit of cover left. To our surprise, song sparrows and swamp sparrows moved back to the burned-over grass as soon as the fire had passed. We also got a very long close look at a rare Le Conte's sparrow that poked around the charred stems, seemingly unaware or uncomprehending that its protective cover had vanished.

The many winter sparrows we flushed from the rail fields often arrive en masse by late October. Early on a sunny morning along a dike surrounding one of the rail fields, I encountered perhaps several hundred swamp sparrows spread out through the hemp sesbania and giant foxtail grass that lined the dike. The dark, plain-breasted sparrows perched on the brown, leafless stems of the sesbania as they leaned over to pick at the green foxtail seed heads bent double from the morning's heavy dew. Additional birds popped up into view with my every "pish" as I walked the dike, the rising sun in my eyes. Many song sparrows with their distinctive chips joined the swamp sparrows, along with a few common yellowthroats and sedge wrens. Some of the sparrows probably had just stopped for a day or so before moving farther south, but many would stay until spring, spreading out and dispersing to other wetland edges throughout the ACE. A few of the song sparrows attempted a rather tentative version of their spring song. Some birds occasionally sing at this time of year, perhaps because day length in October exactly matches that of the April nesting season, and the changing length of daylight has such a profound influence on bird behavior.

Above the dikes and fields, the sky that morning seemed alive with the white and green flashing flight of tree swallows, which follow on the heels of the rough-winged swallows I had seen regularly for a couple of months. By winter, the rough wings would vanish to the south, but tree swallows remain all winter, subsisting on wax myrtle berries when bitter cold grounds flying insects, which make up 80 percent of the birds' diet. Several flocks of fifty or so fish crows, their nasal calls marking their passage overhead, served as another reminder that winter loomed not far ahead. Another late fall arrival, double-crested cormorants, flew overhead in long, disorganized formations, gliding down into open water across the ACE Basin. Virtually absent during the summer and early fall, cormorants become a winter fixture, largely replacing the similar-looking anhingas, most of which move farther south in the winter.

Like much of the ACE Basin, Bear Island comes alive with birds in the fall. Summer's production goes to seed in autumn, and the wetlands, filled with small fishes and invertebrates, along with the brushy dikes pull in a great variety of birds from the northern breeding grounds. Suddenly, small flocks of coots dabble in every pond corner. Little armadas of ruddy ducks, their stumpy tails cocked confidently, cruise the quiet, shallow waters, along with pairs of shovelers, the males green and white, paddling low on the surface. I watched flock after flock of white ibises glide in from a nocturnal roost to settle along a bulrush edge where they began to forage in tight formation, their collective murmuring grunts permeating the still morning air.

The windswept freshwater fields along the Edisto River, during summer devoid of bird life save for painted buntings and marsh wrens, by November have become a swirl of activity with flocks of restless ducks and red-winged black birds silhouetted across the open sky. The myriad sparrows and other songbirds that flit low across the dikes or forage deep among the snowy blooming groundsel bushes and hemp sesbania attract coursing harriers and stealthy Cooper's and sharp-shinned hawks, while red tails circle high above and bald eagles sit expectantly on open perches. I watched a great egret with a six-inch mullet flopping in its yellow beak land awkwardly on the top of a groundsel tree, white with bloom. The egret struggled to maneuver the slippery fish into swallowing position without dropping it, finally succeeding with a convulsive stretch of its long neck. From the dense canopy of a lone cypress tree, a great-horned owl, disturbed from its daytime roost, flapped across the grasslands toward a distant wooded high spot. Come nightfall, when the hawks retire, owls take over patrolling these wetlands, giving the small birds and mammals little respite.

Although the deer hunting season in South Carolina lasts until the end of December, on the three state wildlife management areas, deer hunting ends in November or early December. Of the three, Botany Bay Plantation—with fifty-three days, about half that of an early archery season—offers the most hunting opportunities during the year. However, hunters on the 3,363-acre property took only 32 deer, just 15 of those bucks. Bear Island WMA allowed deer hunting on eighteen days during the fall, and hunters took 23 deer. Donnelley WMA's 8,000 acres provide excellent deer habitat, and hunters there bagged 95 deer on eighteen hunting days during October and November. Collectively, the three properties, totaling 24,000 acres, provide opportunities throughout most of the fall for the deer hunting public, especially important to the many hunters who have few other local areas to hunt. However, hunters on these lands took only 150 deer for the season, about average for the last few years. Some private lands in the ACE Basin receive considerable deer hunting pressure, others not as much. While the harvest fluctuates from year to year, deer, with no other large predators to threaten them, seem quite capable of sustaining the annual harvest. Incidental to the deer harvest, these hunters killed eight feral hogs but no coyotes, although in recent years, deer hunters across South Carolina reported killing thirty thousand coyotes annually. Locally, landowners and property managers occasionally see coyotes, and certainly they roamed all across the ACE Basin but not in large enough numbers for deer hunters to regularly encounter them.

By mid-November, fall colors gradually change the ACE Basin's look, in some years a more pronounced change than in others. While not as spectacular as in New England, the ACE Basin's reds and yellows of autumn often catch the low, soft light of fall's crisp, clear weather with vivid displays. Hickories turn bright, festive yellow, joined by yellow-and-red popcorn trees. A more subtle rusty red invades sweet gums' leaves, and red maples, among the first to lose their leaves, often turn flaming red. Pokeweed, with their leaves long gone, stand along the dikes and roadsides as stark, red skeletons. Suddenly, groundsel trees everywhere begin to shed their seeds, which drift across the wetlands like blowing snow and coat the dikes with a dusting of white.

A dry fall with little rainfall rendered the Salkehatchie River a narrow stream just waist deep in some spots. Sloughs that just a month before held

Southern red oaks line the road to Fields Point. *Pete Laurie.*

several feet of water now lay dry, dotted with little forests of cypress knees, dark and foreboding except for their brownish, growing tops. One such slough, a long arching horseshoe-shaped scar near Ross Catterton's river house, clearly marked a former main channel of the river. Slow-moving coastal rivers, such as the Salkehatchie, meander across a broad flood plain, constantly eroding the soft substrate into sharp bends that regularly cut through narrow spots to take a more direct path. In some swamps, these cut-away loops form oxbow lakes, but along the Salkehatchie, any standing water soon percolates into the sugar sand base.

On the day I visited, the river itself ran the color of strong tea, the recent dry spell providing little runoff upstream to muddy the flow. The low water had exposed old tree trunks and limbs that the generally quiet stream lacks the power to dislodge even at high water. Some of this debris may have fallen into the river decades ago and remained submerged most of that time in the oxygen-poor water, which slows decomposition. Winter rains would soon bring the river back to normal flow or even well out of the channel and up into the flood plain, where it sometimes persists for months. Cypress needles had turned dull brown and started to fall, adding a finer texture to the forest litter and leaving the treetops characteristically "bald" for the coming winter. Bald cypress and other swamp trees survive in this anaerobic soil by developing very shallow root systems, making them easily uprooted by sudden gusts of wind.

While stressful for many plants, the flood plain provides excellent habitat for many invertebrates, especially in the more frequently flooded depressions, where insect larvae, amphipods, worms, snails and clams may exist at densities of thousands of individuals per square foot. These attract larger invertebrates, such as crayfish, and with an extensive flood more than fifty species of fish fan out across the flood plain to forage in the greatly expanded aquatic zone. The most abundant fish species in the Salkehatchie and swamps like it include spotted sucker, bowfin, flat bullhead, largemouth bass, carp, longnose gar, American eel and redbreast. After the river retreats to its normal channel, fishermen enjoy excellent redbreast fishing, with the fish large and fat from weeks or even months of feeding in the productive flood plain. When the river rises, expansion into the flood plain prevents a large slug of fresh water from surging downstream and suddenly reducing the salinity, which would stress many estuarine animals.

Unlike the marshes miles downstream, the swamp in late fall had a hushed tone with little bird activity. Two white-throated sparrows picked among the weed seeds on a high spot close to the quiet river while a row of fresh little holes on the trunk of a water oak indicated the presence of a sapsucker, but the bird stayed out of sight. Toward dusk, as thunder rumbled off to the west and the first winds of an approaching cold front sent down a spiral of leaves, wood ducks whistled from downriver and forty white ibises on their way to roost glided past just above the treetops still lit by the setting sun. In the faltering light, a single bat appeared and began to crisscross an opening, although flying insects seemed scarce.

Weeks later, just before Thanksgiving, a couple days of rain brought down the leaves in torrents. All across the ACE Basin, sweet gums, red maples, hickories and oaks jettisoned their bright foliage while the loblolly and longleaf pines dropped their brown needles. Sandy roads through the uplands became blanketed with a layer of leaves and pine needles. Red oaks—sometimes with a two-tone look of part yellow, part orange—stood in contrast with the perennially green pines. Hardwoods turned yellow above with the autumn leaves of hickory and beech while the understory of red bay and switch cane remained green. Ross told me he had to drive through a foot of water across the river bottom to reach the house, which remained dry on an island of slightly higher ground. The sloughs we had walked just a couple weeks earlier now had flooded, bringing flocks of wood ducks that called and whistled throughout the night as they foraged for submerged acorns. The transition period of fall had settled into winter.

WINTER

By December, with fall migration completed, an entire new suite of bird species has replaced many of the breeding birds of spring and summer, many of the latter having left for points south. With the exception of a very few winter nesters, such as bald eagles and great-horned owls, the winter residents, arriving in fits and starts throughout the fall, come primarily to eat. Upland birds seek seeds, nuts, berries and overwintering insect eggs and larvae. The water birds come looking for unfrozen, open water with native plants, fishes and small invertebrates. Of the 280 species of birds that regularly spend part of the year in the ACE Basin, only 90 have permanent resident status. Another 90 species, including 28 species of waterfowl, spend only the winter months in the ACE. Bird behavior also changes with the seasons. By winter, the stealthy, guarded behavior and territorial bickering of the breeding season vanishes, as many birds join noisy, restless flocks that roam unpredictably across the landscape. Some flocks consist of a single species, while others have a mixed population sometimes of unexpected and unrelated birds. With much of the growing season's foliage withered and fallen to the ground, birds lose their cover and become more visible. All of these facts make winter the ACE Basin birdwatcher's favorite season.

Winter's early morning sun illuminates an immature red-shouldered hawk at Bear Island WMA. *Pete Laurie.*

But long before bird watching became a popular hobby, the fascination with duck hunting and the passion it inspired among the wealthy rescued the abandoned rice plantations, kept these large properties intact as hunting preserves and laid the foundations of the ACE Basin Project. Today, duck hunting remains a central focus of the ACE Basin, with most wetlands, both public and private, intensively managed throughout the year to set the table for the many species of waterfowl that arrive in late fall and remain until spring.

After all the time and effort wetland managers put into attracting ducks for the winter, once hunting season starts, they have the conflicting problem of providing as much good shooting as possible while still holding the ducks. Some private property owners hunt their ducks regularly throughout the season while others hunt more casually. Public lands receive a great demand for hunting opportunities, and the hunting public expects to see lots of ducks and have a chance for a successful hunt. The ACE Basin's premier public waterfowl hunting area, Bear Island Wildlife Management Area, has developed a successful balance that offers as much public waterfowl hunting as possible while providing an enjoyable experience for all hunters. Individuals wishing to hunt at Bear Island must apply well in advance of the season and pay a fee. A computer randomly selects sixteen hunters per day with hunts conducted on Tuesdays, Thursdays and Saturdays during the December through January season. To spread out the hunting pressure over Bear Island's 4,800 acres of managed wetlands and to give ducks time and space to rest and feed, the Bear Island staff rotates hunting among three sites: the West Side on Tuesdays, the East Side on Thursdays and the Springfield/ Cut area on Saturdays. With eighty blinds throughout the three areas, staff can place two hunters to a blind with plenty of space between them.

On a Bear Island duck hunt, the hunters arrive well before daylight and receive a briefing on the rules and regulations as well as the federally mandated bag limits. In recent years, federal regulations have restricted hunters to a total of six ducks per day, with further limitations by species. Bear Island staff provide transport to the selected hunting area, dropping each pair of hunters on the dike adjacent to a blind. Hunters then load their gear in a provided aluminum johnboat and paddle out to the blind. Some hunters bring their own decoys to supplement the dozen provided. Before first light, hunters set out the decoys around the blind and get ready to call in passing flocks of ducks. Each hunter can take no more than twenty-five shotgun shells to the blind and must use a shotgun that holds no more than three rounds. Federal regulations also require waterfowl hunters throughout the country to use only nontoxic (not lead) shot. At nine o'clock, Bear Island staff drive the dike past each blind. Those hunters with their limit of birds or who have shot all their shells or have become cold and wet can elect to end their hunt at that time. Most, however, stay for the final pickup at 10:30 a.m. With this schedule, on any hunt day, Bear Island waterfowl, spread across the entire property, get shot at by sixteen hunters for about three hours. As a result, hunters enjoy a rewarding experience without impacting the overall duck population.

On a couple mornings, I rode with Ross Catterton as he picked up the hunters. Bear Island in winter takes on a wilder feel, with long skeins of tundra swans, necks stretched far ahead of their bodies, winging well above the wetlands, where bunched flocks of white pelicans mill on the surface. The haunting calls of the swans mixed with a sudden cackle of moorhen, the piercing whistle of a yellowlegs on the wing or the hoarse squawk of a startled egret create a sense of wildness that only Bear Island in winter can impart. Around every twist of the dike, we encountered wildlife. A passing eagle sent a flock of five hundred coots pattering into the corner of an impoundment with the roar of one thousand webbed feet. Strings of white ibises in neat lines alternately flapped and glided overhead in perfect

Tundra swans spend winter nights at the house pond at Bear Island WMA, dispersing to adjacent wetlands to feed throughout the day. *Phillip Jones.*

unison. A bobcat bounded across a dike, and a great-horned owl twisted around to watch us approach before spreading its broad wings to vanish into a copse of live oak. Rounding one corner, we flushed six roseate spoonbills, pale pink complements to the mostly all-white egrets and ibises. Cooper's hawks, ready to pounce on a careless song sparrow or yellow throat, cruised low on set wings along the dike edges. Kingfishers perched alertly on trunk uprights, and above them, tree swallows wheeled and swooped on the few mosquitoes lured from their winter slumber by the warm, humid breeze of early winter. And everywhere we saw ducks—shovelers tipping to reach the widgeon grass below, gadwall in great flocks leaping into the air as one, wary pintails flashing white as they started to pitch in then flared abruptly and changed direction.

At each blind, the hunters greeted us with broad smiles and detailed stories of success as they loaded their decoys and guns into the back of the pickup and proudly hoisted their feathered trophies, now just limp and lifeless, each a testimony to their marksmanship and hunting prowess and most destined to provide excellent table fare. Back at the check station, Ross and his staff recorded the number and species of each duck killed, how many ducks the hunters shot but could not retrieve and the number of shots fired. On one morning, fifteen hunters took eighty-five ducks on 293 shots with only seven lost birds—a very good hunt. More remarkable, the bag that morning included ten different species. Gadwall, the most abundant duck at Bear

Island at the time, led the way with twenty-three birds. The remainder of the harvest consisted of widgeon, pintail, shoveler, mottled duck, ruddy duck, both green-winged and blue-winged teal and two unexpected extras: a hen canvasback and, even more surprising, a hen golden-eye. In the previous year, hunters at Bear Island had taken only two canvasbacks all season, and the only golden-eye reported killed in the entire state that year came from a wildlife management area far inland. Golden-eye hens have such a nondescript plumage that the staff at first identified the bird as a ruddy duck until they noted its much greater size.

The success of that day's hunt—5.6 birds per hunter—and the diversity of species taken attested to the yearlong effort Bear Island staff put into the day-to-day management practices that make this area the top public waterfowl hunting spot in the state. Ross and his crew get as much satisfaction from a successful hunt as the hunters do themselves.

However, not all hunts have such a high ratio of ducks to hunter. The following day, thirteen hunters in the Springfield/Cut portion of Bear Island bagged just forty-two ducks of five species. Weather conditions had not changed, except that the good breeze of the first day had vanished by the second day. Of course, the experience and expertise of individual hunters varies considerably from one hunt to the next. On that second day when Bear Island hunters had only modest success, a very good hunter in a blind on private property adjacent to Bear Island killed his limit of six ducks, in this case all gadwalls, in less than fifteen minutes. "Took me longer to put out the decoys," he said, adding that he had shot just thirteen times.

Certainly, the carefully controlled hunting at places like Bear Island and the restrictive bag limits set each year by the U.S. Fish and Wildlife Service ensure that hunters make only a small dent in overall waterfowl populations. In a recent year, 282 hunters at Bear Island bagged 1,130 ducks of seventeen species during the entire season, perhaps 2 or 3 percent of ducks that wintered there. Multiply that by the ninety-one thousand acres of impoundments and natural wetlands in the ACE Basin, much of that receiving little hunting pressure, and the impact of hunting becomes negligible. Conditions on waterfowl breeding grounds in the plains of the Midwest and the Canadian provinces and subsequent nesting success have a far greater influence on annual waterfowl populations than does hunting in the fall and winter. Sufficient rainfall in recent years has kept the critically important prairie potholes filled, producing ideal nesting conditions for many species. As a result, waterfowl populations across the continent have reached historically high levels, at least since record keeping began in the 1940s.

Red-cockaded woodpeckers excavate nest cavities in living trees and peck through the surrounding bark to generate a protective flow of sap that discourages predators. *Phillip Jones.*

While a number of species of birds have naturally expanded their ranges into the ACE Basin in the past twenty-five years, biologists recently have gone to great lengths to bring back a species whose range long ago contracted to such an extent that it vanished from the ACE. The red-cockaded woodpecker once roamed throughout the Southeast's estimated ninety million acres of almost unbroken longleaf pine, one of the most extensive forests that ever existed. These habitat-specific and non-adaptable woodpeckers evolved over the centuries to thrive in mature yellow pines of open woodlands, the undergrowth controlled by fires started by lightning strikes. Eventually, the country's growing demand for lumber and the ability of railroads to penetrate these forests resulted in clear-cutting huge swaths of the bird's habitat such that almost all of it had disappeared by the middle of the twentieth century. Unable to adapt to this loss of habitat, red-cockaded woodpeckers declined dramatically across their once extensive range. The U.S. Fish and Wildlife Service declared the bird endangered in the 1970s.

Red-cockaded woodpeckers, which live in colonies of four to eight birds, usually family members, require at least seventy-five acres of pines thirty years or more old and with a minimal hardwood understory controlled by frequent fires. Today, such areas exist in many scattered places throughout the Southeast, including the ACE Basin, but the woodpeckers, having evolved in an environment where they never needed to colonize distant habitats, no matter how suitable, never seem to find these isolated areas. As a result, much of the bird's population exists in relatively few large areas of mature southern yellow pine, such as the Francis Marion National Forest north of Charleston. Hurricane Hugo, which in 1989 destroyed much of that forest and, with it, a lot of prime red-cockaded habitat, showed the need to spread out the birds so that a single natural disaster would not threaten the bird's remnant populations. Because of the bird's endangered status and because red-cockaded woodpeckers excavate cavities in living, not dead, trees, many private landowners do not want red-cockaded on their property, fearing the presence of an endangered species might restrict the amount of timber they could harvest. However, a couple of ACE Basin landowners have welcomed the reintroduction of these birds. They view red-cockaded woodpeckers as a historic part of the ecosystem and consider the birds an asset, not a liability.

One morning in early December, I arrived at Nemours Plantation on the Combahee River shortly after daylight as a group of federal biologists, working with a private contractor, released four red-cockaded woodpeckers from artificial cavities that the contractor had placed earlier in two stands of mature pines. They had captured the birds the previous evening in their roost cavities, transported them to Nemours and placed them in the manufactured cavities with screens to prevent them from escaping during the night. Three birds, including a mated pair, had come from a private tract

A red-cockaded woodpecker artificial nest cavity insert, carefully disguised to appear natural, at Nemours Plantation. *Pete Laurie.*

near Myrtle Beach scheduled for development; the fourth bird came from a colony in the Francis Marion.

Nemours biologist Beau Bauer and I went to look at the new colonies, each of which consisted of four artificial cavities, inserted into the trunks of mature pines, with two birds introduced into each colony, the first in longleaf pine about eight hundred yards from the second in shortleaf pine. The inserts, at a height of twenty to thirty feet above the ground, all faced southwest, the orientation normally selected by the birds themselves. The contractor had installed the inserts weeks earlier by carving a rectangular hole just the size of the insert into the tree trunk, wedging the insert securely into the hole and then painting the exterior to make it look as natural as possible. The installer had even hacked a few holes through the bark above and to the sides of the hole. The pine resin oozing from the holes, along with a few streaks of white paint, gave the tree the look of a real cavity tree, which the birds turn white by pecking holes through the bark and allowing the sap to run down the trunk. Sticky sap around the nest hole may deter predators such as raccoons and snakes.

Bauer said as soon as the biologists had pulled the screens out of the way at daybreak, the birds flew out of their new homes and, with considerable calling back and forth, vanished into the surrounding forest. An hour later, we saw no birds at either colony, although their normal behavior takes them away from the colony during much of the day as they forage for insects. Toward dusk they return to the colony to roost for the night. Bauer planned to check out each colony at sunset after the birds had a few days to become acclimated.

A week later, I visited a second series of new red-cockaded woodpecker colonies, this one at Chehaw-Combahee Plantation, where the same reintroduction program had brought in ten pairs of birds after installing forty inserts. All of these birds came from different colonies within the Francis Marion, in an attempt to improve genetic diversity as well as spread the birds into vacant portions of their historic range. Plantation manager Lew Crouch took time from his busy schedule to drive me to five of his new colonies on the twelve-thousand-acre property. At our first stop, we had barely gotten out of the truck when Lew heard one of the woodpeckers. A few minutes later, we saw it flying between the scattered pines at the colony, and then we saw the second bird of this pair. Both seemed to have acclimated to their new surroundings. In addition, we noted freshly pecked holes around all four of the inserts, suggesting that the new residents had accepted these artificial cavities and had begun their normal modifications. The cavity inserts play a key role in the success of the reintroduction program since it takes a red-cockaded up to two years to excavate a roost/nest cavity on its own. Other woodpeckers, working on the softer, partially decayed wood of dead trees, can carve out a cavity in just a couple of weeks, generally creating a new one every time they nest. Red-cockaded woodpeckers, after all the time and effort they have invested, use their laboriously constructed cavities for years, probably for several generations. Releasing birds into areas without cavities would doom them to try surviving without shelter from the elements and predators and with nowhere to successfully breed for a couple of years.

Although relocating plants and animals to new geographical areas often results in major and unforeseen problems, moving these woodpeckers to new areas should cause no problems since the birds once lived in this same habitat. The reintroduced red-cockaded will not bring in any new diseases or parasites, nor will it compete adversely with native animals. Natural predators and other factors will keep the birds in balance with the habitat. The woodpeckers lived here before, albeit probably almost one hundred years ago, and should fit right back into the ecosystem with no unexpected or unwanted side effects. Nor will the presence of such a limited number of birds on these large properties have any impact on timber harvest in the foreseeable future.

At the four other new colonies that Lew and I visited, we did not hear or see any red-cockaded woodpeckers, but in all but one colony, the four trees with inserts had fresh peck marks around the entrances, an indication that the birds had accepted the artificial cavities. The soft December afternoon sun, the temperature a comfortable sixty-five degrees and just a hint of a breeze rendered the quiet winter woods most enjoyable as we tramped among these new colonies, ears straining to catch the red-cockaded's distinctive call note and our binoculars at the ready. The federal contractors had selected a stand of slash pine for one of the new colonies; the others they had established in longleaf pine. The birds apparently have no preference for species among the southern yellow pines. Throughout the area we covered, the habitat consisted of classic well-managed southern pine, with scattered trees of fifty to sixty years of age with an understory of waist-high sweet gum and turkey oak, the latter still holding brown withered leaves. Big longleaf cones lay scattered on the sandy soil and occasionally crunched underfoot. Crouch said he planned to burn much of the area in the spring, in his regular rotation of burning the property's pinelands every two years.

Red-cockaded woodpeckers play a vital role in southern pine environment since they have the ability to create cavities. Many other birds and animals, incapable of carving out their own cavities, become secondary users of the woodpeckers' laboriously constructed roosts. At least twenty-seven species of vertebrates—including, snakes, lizards, squirrels, frogs and other birds—plus a variety of insects use these cavities. So the reintroduction of these birds not only returns a natural inhabitant to ACE Basin uplands but also adds a long-absent but important element to the complex food web of these forests. If these first colonies become successfully established and additional private landowners welcome the birds, the iconic red-cockaded woodpecker may once again become a common sight throughout the area.

While the red-cockaded woodpecker's comeback in the ACE has just gotten started, the return of the bald eagle began in the 1970s with great success. Outlawing the use of DDT and other persistent pesticides became the first important step in the recovery of not only eagles but also ospreys, brown pelicans and other avian predators. The widespread overuse of persistent pesticides did not necessarily kill the birds, but they altered the birds' reproductive systems, resulting in thin-shelled eggs that broke as the birds tried to incubate them. Populations declined drastically as reproduction failed year after year.

Eagles also have benefited from strict enforcement of laws against indiscriminate shooting, protection of nest trees and public education efforts. A statewide survey of bald eagles in South Carolina in 1977 located just thirteen nests. Today, more than 250 pairs of eagles nest annually in the state, with many of those nests in the ACE Basin.

Bald eagles start nesting in December, usually using the same nest year after year, adding new material annually until nests become huge and easily visible from a distance. In the ACE Basin, eagles generally select living pines with a sturdy crotch of limbs just below the canopy. Shade from the canopy may help protect the nestlings from direct sun during the months they remain in the nest developing the feathers and muscles needed for flight.

Beau Bauer took me to see an early nesting eagle on a damp, foggy morning at Nemours Plantation. We drove slowly through the maze of dikes between the old rice fields along the Combahee River. Harriers, three or four at a time, ghost-like in the fog, glided ahead of us, teetering side to side on their long wings as they searched the giant cord grass edges for sparrows and other small prey. We finally turned onto a dike that curved back to the mainland. Bauer stopped the truck and pointed to a dark mass in a large loblolly pine. Through binoculars, the nest appeared empty, but a spotting scope allowed us to visibly penetrate the thick fog just enough to make out the white head of an adult eagle, probably the female, sitting on eggs, quite unusual for the first week of December. Bauer, however, said these birds, presumably the same pair, had used this nest for at least ten years and always had eggs by Thanksgiving, a good month ahead of schedule.

Eagles nest in winter in part because of the abundance of prey available at that time of year. While eagles regularly scavenge dead animals, they also can catch fish, waterfowl and a variety of other prey. Coots, usually abundant in the winter and easy to capture, serve as a favorite prey for eagles to feed the young birds in the nest. Coots form large rafts on the shallow impoundments and, unlike ducks, flush only reluctantly. When an eagle appears overhead, the panicked coots dive repeatedly below the surface. When the birds become exhausted and out of breath, the eagle pounces on an easy victim. The large acreage of managed wetlands in the ACE, along with surrounding high ground and mature pines, offers eagles nest sites and abundant prey—in other words, ideal bald eagle nesting habitat. On any winter day in the ACE, an observant person can see

Bald eagles, which mate for life, begin nesting in the ACE Basin in late November or early December. *Phillip Jones.*

a dozen eagles without much effort. A midwinter eagle survey conducted one morning on Bear Island WMA by DNR biologists Dean Harrigal and Christy Hand located seventeen birds, with immatures outnumbering adults. Eagles require four or five years to develop the unmistakable adult plumage of white head and tail, so many of the birds seen in the ACE appear as very large dark birds, usually with some whitish mottling. Occasionally, a bird in juvenile plumage mates with an adult bird and successfully rears chicks. Inexperienced bird watchers often misidentify these immature birds as golden eagles. However, golden eagles, a more western species, only rarely wander as far east as the ACE Basin.

In winter, ACE Basin beaches take on a much milder tone than in summer. The winter sun shines weakly, without the intense heat and harsh glare of July. The often quiet sea rolls in with gentle breakers that slide smoothly up the wet sand, and the clear air allows the viewing of passing freighters and late season shrimp trawlers at work far off on the horizon. On just such a day, I tagged along on the monthly shorebird survey conducted at Botany Bay Wildlife Management Area by DNR's Bess Kellert and a couple of volunteers. Kellert conducts this shorebird survey quite differently than the ones I had experienced with Nick Wallover on the ACE Basin's other uninhabited beaches at Otter and Pine Islands. The beach at Botany Bay allows for easy land access, but only at low tide since the severely eroded strip of sand disappears at high tide, which has eaten completely into the adjacent maritime forest. At low tide, the ocean retreats fifty to one hundred yards, leaving a wide expanse of hard-packed sand. We drove onto this low tide beach in an ATV and turned south, skimming quickly along the upper beach littered with a great variety of shells, the majority well-worn oyster shells. With the tide low, shorebirds of both the beach and adjacent marsh mud flats had dispersed across foraging areas spread over thousands of acres, so we did not expect to see the bunched flocks of birds that congregate on Otter Island at high tide. Still, monthly surveys conducted over many years will give an idea of species composition on Botany Bay and how it changes with the seasons, both useful in increasing our understanding of these key species so sensitive to coastal development, rising sea level and other environmental issues.

The beach that morning seemed devoid of bird life until we reached an area where the eroding beach as it marched inland had exposed the roots of spartina marsh that the sand had overwashed many months earlier. Here, several species of shorebirds foraged actively. Most we identified as dunlins, with their distinctive drooping beaks. Joining them, a few red knots in pale winter plumage and a couple of ruddy turnstones probed this mud flat in the surf. Farther down the beach, we parked the ATV and walked toward Townsend Inlet, which separates Botany Bay from Interlude Beach to the west. Here, the waves and currents had carved the beach into a constantly changing array of shallow tidal pools and curving gouges where the still retreating tide flowed in shallow riverlets from the marsh behind the beach.

The cold, waist-deep water in the inlet blocked our passage, but we set up spotting scopes and counted the birds on Interlude as far as we could

Dunlins in winter plumage forage in the intertidal zone on the beach at Otter Island.
Phillip Jones.

see. Dunlins made up the bulk of these, and once we included the species we had seen earlier, we eventually tallied 130. Most fed actively on the many invertebrates in the mud and sand that only the low tide exposed. We also walked to the top of the shallow ridge of sand that separated the tidal beach from the marsh behind. At the very tip of this long ridge, a small area of shallow dunes still supported a few sea oats and patches of sea croton and salt hay, the last remnants of what just a few years ago constituted a typical dune system. In recent years, as the beach eroded, storm tides regularly washed over this area, destroying all but this last little patch of dunes, which the next big storm might wipe away at high tide by the looks of them.

Survey completed, we cruised back up the beach in the noisy ATV, stopping a couple of times to look just beyond the surf for sea ducks. Several red-throated loons bobbed on the slight roll and then dove smoothly below the surface for thirty seconds or more in search of small fishes. Dark shapes farther out suggested scoters, but we never got a good enough look to determine which of the three species we saw. Closer in, a tight flock of a half dozen buffleheads swam away from us, and through the scopes, we could just barely make out the distinctive shape of gannets wheeling and diving far offshore. All these common winter birds, absent in the summer, make the winter beach that much more interesting.

With many plants dormant in winter and little ground cover, recently dug holes, the work of armadillos and not very noticeable for much of the year, begin to appear in all sorts of upland habitats from agricultural fields to pine savannah. This odd-looking creature, with its armored shell and pointed snout, has simply walked north for the past one hundred years, expanding its once limited range along the Gulf Coast into much of the Southeast. Unheard of locally just fifteen or twenty years ago, the adaptable, omnivorous armadillo has now become a common part of the ACE Basin fauna, although certainly not a welcome part. Armadillos eat primarily ground-dwelling insects and grubs that they unearth with constant digging. They also consume small reptiles, amphibians, mammals and bird eggs— virtually any animal matter they encounter. Most active at night, they retreat during the day to burrows they seem to dig randomly in almost any upland area. With their natural predators, including wolves and cougars, extirpated throughout the Southeast, they have nothing to control their growing and expanding population.

I encountered one of these creatures while searching for winter sparrows along an open stand of mature loblollies on the edge of an old field. A sudden rustle in the sparse understory just twenty feet away caught my attention. I took a couple of steps forward and spotted the distinctive curved back of an armadillo as it turned that sharp little face in my direction, its beady eyes fixed on me suspiciously. In another second, it vanished into a hidden burrow among the leaves and pine straw. I have seldom encountered one of these mostly nocturnal animals, although one time at Donnelley WMA, I crossed paths with four armadillos in twenty minutes within a radius of fifty yards. Hunters, birdwatchers, property managers and others who spend a lot of time in the field see armadillos occasionally during daylight hours. While, to their credit, they consume fire ants, they also probably eat the eggs of ground-nesting birds, including quail, and consume a whole array of snakes, toads and native wildlife, disrupting the natural food web in ways not yet fully recognized.

Many songbirds form winter-foraging flocks consisting of a mixture of species. This behavior concentrates birds in nomadic flocks, leaving the uplands all but devoid of birds over wide areas. One can walk or drive for considerable distance through any ACE Basin property in the winter and encounter virtually no birds at all. Then, suddenly, birds appear everywhere— some scratching in the leaf litter, others gleaning dormant insects and insect eggs from high overhead or snatching poison ivy berries from a dangling vine. These loose flocks generally move slowly across the landscape, staying in touch with quiet chips and calls, even as they forage for different foods in separate parts of the habitat. Typical flocks might consist of white-throated sparrows, cardinals, pine and yellow-throated warblers, chickadees, titmice, gold finches, ruby-crowned kinglets and white-breasted nuthatches, along with one or two downy or red-bellied woodpeckers and perhaps a solitary vireo or a couple golden-crowned kinglets. Such concentrations can include virtually every songbird in an area of many acres, all in one place. The ACE Basin's extensive, unbroken woodlands offer far superior habitat for these foraging flocks than developed suburban areas. Just exactly what these diverse species gain from forming these foraging flocks remains unclear, as each species seeks different foods. Many pairs of eyes may better spot the approach of predators such as sharp-shinned hawks, but the constant motion of such active flocks almost certainly attracts predators as well. Moreover, some of these birds seek out often scarce cavities to spend the night and probably compete with one another for such roosting places.

Interestingly, yellow-rumped warblers, among the commonest of winter songbirds in the ACE, seldom join these mixed-species flocks. Instead, they roam the woodlands and hedgerows in their own separate, active flocks, their distinctive chips and flashing, buttery rumps a traditional part of the winter experience. Some years, this northern migrant becomes so numerous and ubiquitous as to overwhelm the uplands, making it difficult to locate any other species. Along the edges, bluebirds, which also often form their own flocks, sometimes join the yellow rumps, although the bluebirds, as thrushes, have no close relation to the warblers.

Another member of the thrush family, robins also form single-species winter flocks, crisscrossing forested wetlands and deep swamps of the ACE Basin in search of wild fruit and berries. The symbol of spring throughout most of North America but a winter bird in the ACE, robins only in recent decades have started nesting along the South Carolina coast and still in small, isolated pockets. Robins that breed inland and to the north arrive in the ACE during the fall and by winter have gathered into nomadic flocks that may include hundreds of birds. Few people ever see robins during the winter because they shun suburban lawns, retreating instead to the remotest woodlands and forested swamps, where they feed on the fruit of American holly, yaupon, blackgum, water tupelo, palmetto, dogwood, chinaberry and privet. In late winter, they emerge from the swamps and change both their diet and behavior as they spread north and west with the advancing spring.

One late afternoon, I watched a winter flock of robins converge on a small swamp dominated by water tupelo. The birds streamed in from a pine-hardwood ridge in groups of four or five and attacked the teardrop-shaped tupelo berries with noisy calls and great fluttering of wings. The entire little swamp suddenly became a whirl of flashing wings and red breasts from the top of the leafless canopy to the wet forest floor around the buttressed trunks. At least two hundred robins, acting not at all like the relaxed fixtures of suburban lawns, hung upside down from the tips of the tupelo branches plucking the fruit or flew randomly in all directions. The disorganized flock contained no other species during the fifteen minutes I watched the performance and might not pass that way again all winter.

Winter's cold sends the ACE Basin's abundant alligators into dens for much of the season. As coldblooded reptiles, they cannot control their internal temperature, which subsequently fluctuates with water temperature. When that temperature dips below about seventy degrees, they stop feeding and remain dormant in dens they dig into the banks and dikes along the edges of wetlands. On warm, sunny days they might emerge to bask on the bank or to float on the water's surface but they do not feed from November to March. Researchers estimate that over the course of a year an eight-hundred-pound alligator eats less than a one-hundred-pound dog. This ability to thrive on very little food relative to size allows coldblooded predators, including gators, to develop the high-density populations typical of ACE wetlands. With many non-blood relatives within each individual's home range, gators do not suffer from inbreeding and can maintain a healthy, genetically diverse population, which has no doubt contributed to their success over millions of years.

The alligators' long winter fast coincides nicely with the influx of wintering waterfowl. While gators eat just about anything that gets in, on or near the water, including ducks, by the time water temperature climbs above seventy degrees in the spring, most waterfowl have already flown north to the breeding grounds. Throughout the winter, the thousands of ducks that inhabit ACE Basin wetlands have little to fear from the abundant gators. By the same token, duck hunters can confidently send their retrievers into the water to fetch downed birds without much worry that the dog will fall prey to a gator. During the remainder of the year, gators, while little threat to humans, generally grab any dog foolish enough to venture near the water.

One winter day in a stand of mixed oak and pine, I came upon a recently wind-thrown red oak. The big hardwood had taken out several loblolly pines as it crashed down. A yellow-throated warbler, the sun gleaming on the bright breeding plumage it keeps all year long, poked among the bark of the tree's prone trunk. Holes in the canopy created by blown-down trees create sunny openings that allow understory plants to gain a foothold. Many of these keep their foliage throughout the winter, providing a layer of decorative green among the starkly bare trunks and branches of the deciduous trees. These woody, evergreen species include red bay, switch cane, cross vine, magnolia, American holly, yaupon and dwarf palmetto.

The same winter storm that had toppled the red oak had also broken off two nearby long dead pines that time had reduced to just bare stubs, devoid of both limbs and bark. Now lying prostrate among the bracken ferns, the rotted trunks contained numerous perfectly round holes, three-eighths of an inch in diameter, all neatly carved out by carpenter bees. Resembling bumblebees, carpenter bees do not eat wood, but they gnaw into dead limbs, tree trunks and structural wood, creating long chambers where the female bees lay eggs and rear young. Carpenter bees overwinter as adults, so each hole in these pine logs probably contained a dormant bee waiting for a warm April day to emerge, mate and start another generation.

Twenty-five years ago, I started the ACE Basin Christmas Bird Count as a way to generate information on populations of winter birds and how they change over the years, as well as to introduce more people to the recreational opportunities of the ACE. The National Audubon Society coordinates Christmas counts, now held in several thousand places all across North America. Counts must take place within a week or so on either side of Christmas and within a designated fifteen-mile-diameter circle. I centered the circle at Brickyard Bridge where Bennetts Point Road crosses the Ashepoo River. The circle includes much of the National Estuarine Research Reserve, all of Bear Island WMA, about half of Donnelley WMA and most of the Hollings ACE Basin National Wildlife Refuge. The circle also encompasses a number of prominent private plantations, including Ashepoo, Lavington and Chehaw-Combahee, the owners of which generously allow birdwatchers on their property for the daylong count.

On a warm, overcast morning, the Sunday after Christmas, I led our usual party of four birders through the side gate into the southern half of Donnelley WMA. As always, we tried to visit the most productive bird spots throughout our territory, recording every species we could identify by sight or sound, and at least estimate how many individual birds of each species we saw. Both species and numbers can vary considerably from year to year, which make bird counts both challenging and interesting. Weather conditions obviously play a key role. Cold, blustery days, especially those with heavy rain, keep birds hunkered down out of sight and make conditions unpleasant for the watchers. On sunny days, most upland birds cease activity by midmorning, making afternoons very slow and unproductive. But with the sky overcast and a hint of possible rain, we expected a good count.

A singing pine warbler, one of those permanent residents that seem to sing all year long, stopped us inside the gate to sort through a small group of common species, including white-breasted nuthatch, chipping sparrow, downy woodpecker and yellow-rumped warbler. Against the gray sky, well above the tops of the tall loblolly pines, we could see the silhouettes of robins, scores of them, streaming south in scattered little groups, perhaps migrants that had flown all night and were still not ready to stop. A little later, we recorded several hundred robins in the bush-hogged dove fields near the tractor shed. Recent rains had left these fields with large, shallow puddles in the low spots, attracting the omnivorous robins to invertebrates flushed from the saturated soil. Some years, we do not see a single robin at Donnelley during the count, but we tallied 275 by the day's end, almost all of them in planted fields, not the wooded swamps where I had seen them just two day before.

Some birds we found in traditional spots in expected numbers. In one impoundment with several high spots grown up in myrtle bushes and groundsel trees, the usual contingent of about twenty black-crowned night herons, half still in streaky juvenile plumage, roosted for the day after a night of foraging for small fishes and invertebrates. On the far end of the same impoundment, thirty white pelicans in a tight flock milled about on the surface, their big yellow beaks sweeping small organisms from the shallow water. Fifteen years ago, white pelicans in the ACE Basin would have astounded us; today, we expect to see them all winter and in considerable numbers. Christmas counts held in the same area year after year help to document these types of range extensions and other shifts in bird movements.

Bird identification requires as much listening as looking. Throughout the count day, one or another of our field party would suddenly pause, point in some direction and say knowingly "downy woodpecker" or "brown-headed nuthatch" or "catbird." Most of these we never attempted to actually see, since the call serves to positively identify the caller. We knew our best chance to add secretive species to our list depended almost solely on hearing a distinctive call in the right habitat. In a freshwater wetland where we knew several species of elusive rails might prowl, we played recorded calls and got a sora rail to answer but heard nothing from the Virginia and king rails we had hoped might also respond. When approaching thick undergrowth or grassy edges along dikes, a quiet, lisping hiss will sometimes prompt secretive winter songbirds to pop from cover, if only for a second or two. Such hissing

White pelicans do not dive, feeding instead on small organisms near the surface, usually in large groups. *Phillip Jones.*

can entice common yellowthroats, sedge wrens and many species of sparrows into view, birds that might otherwise stay well hidden.

Annual counts demonstrate dramatically how bird numbers can change in any given year in the same habitats. On some Christmas counts at Donnelley, we record a handful of ducks, mostly wood ducks. But we flushed just a single pair of wood ducks that exploded from a grassy, flooded field with a raucous "woo-eck." What we lacked in wood ducks we more than made up for in gadwalls, a common winter duck throughout the ACE Basin but not generally abundant at Donnelley. On most of the previous twenty-four Christmas counts at Donnelley, we have rarely seen more than a handful of gadwall, and many years none at all. But on this warm, muggy day, we recorded an estimated 450 during the day, most in two large flocks, feeding on widgeon grass. We also counted 150 white ibises during the day, much higher numbers than normal but not unexpected. For birds in large, mobile flocks, birdwatchers have no time to count individual birds and instead rely on estimates based on experience.

Several normally common birds we had difficulty locating on the count. Of cardinals, white-throated sparrows and yellow-rumped warblers—all generally abundant across most upland habitats during the winter—we recorded just small numbers. Some years we see large flocks of fish crows, but we never saw or heard a fish crow all day. As we paused for lunch at a picnic table outside the check station, we had sixty-eight species, a pretty decent tally for the morning, though with many common species still missing. Before we moved on, we walked behind the nearby tractor shed and workshop and, as usual, located a little group of slate-colored juncos, a rather uncommon winter migrant that we see almost every year in this same spot but never anywhere else.

To have a good count, we needed to "get" as many of the common species as possible, plus a few uncommon species—or better yet, a couple of totally unexpected species. Subtle changes in habitat, as well as variables in weather both locally and farther north, combined with a little luck sometimes produce these not-often-seen species. As we drove or walked through several easily accessible forested wetlands, we searched for rusty blackbirds, a usually habitat-specific species. We eventually saw a total of seventeen, just where we expected them. Water pipits we recorded in their typical habitat of open fields. On the other hand, we unexpectedly located a quite uncommon orange-crowned warbler, a bird that normally stays on or near the ground, in a clump of mistletoe at the top of a water tupelo. Late in the afternoon, we got the day's best bird, vesper sparrows, in a loose flock of about ten along a weedy fence row. We had not recorded a vesper sparrow, an uncommon winter visitor from the west, in twenty years.

By late in the day, with the temperature an unseasonal seventy-five degrees, a few mosquitoes had emerged from their winter stupor, and in wet spots, chorus frogs had begun to call. Toward dusk, the warm, wet weather had spring peepers tuning up. Donnelley's abundant alligators, often out of sight on Christmas counts, emerged here and there to float on mats of vegetation or bask in what little sun the day afforded. We even sent an armadillo scampering through the leaf litter and lingering puddles of a low, wooded spot. As the daylight faded, we gave up on seeing any turkeys, even though we knew Donnelley supported several flocks of the big birds. Just before we drove out the gate, we stopped in the road to listen for owls, finally hearing the distant slurred call of a barred owl. In the gathering twilight, we got the last bird of the day, a hermit thrush that we could hear but not see in the dark woods. Our total at Donnelley for the Christmas Bird Count stood at ninety-four species of 2,623 individuals, one of our highest species totals ever.

The entire ACE Christmas Count totaled 144 species, about average. Ducks made up the four most abundant species on the count. Widgeon led the way with more than 17,000 individuals, and pintails, gadwall and green-winged teal all topped 10,000. Counters also recorded 6,800 coots. These numbers reflect the success of the intense management practices that go into attracting and holding winter waterfowl. Also, birdwatchers on Christmas counts concentrate their efforts around wetlands, which provide habitat not just for waterfowl but also for wading birds, shorebirds and the raptors that feed on all these water birds. By contrast, upland habitats in the winter support far fewer birds, and those often cluster in foraging flocks that birders sometimes have difficulty finding. The count's most abundant upland species included red-winged blackbirds (1,804), yellow-rumped warblers (1,763) and robins (1,126), all of which roam across the ACE Basin throughout the winter in flocks. The recently imported red-cockaded woodpeckers made their first appearance on the count, as did rosette spoonbills, a few of which now hang around all winter along the South Carolina coast. Other unusual species included a single sandhill crane in a plantation horse lot and a Krider's hawk, the rare almost-white color phase of the red-tailed hawk.

While winter remained mild through Christmas, a sudden cold snap in early January dropped nighttime temperatures into the teens and low twenties. Duck hunters did not seem to mind, but cold winter weather always draws the nervous attention of commercial shrimpers and recreational fishermen. White shrimp, the mainstay of South Carolina's commercial catch, overwinter in shallow coastal waters. Long-term record keeping by the DNR's Marine Division has shown that when water temperature drops to forty-six degrees or below and remains that low for seven or more days, the cold can wipe out almost all the white shrimp brood stock needed in the following spring. With a poor shrimp spawn in May and early June, the subsequent commercial harvest of white shrimp for that year plummets.

Cold coastal waters send shrimp and fish into deep holes, where the water can remain slightly warmer. Prolonged cold spells can decimate not just shrimp but some recreational fish species as well, notably spotted seatrout, resulting in below-normal recreational fishing for several years until the stocks can recover. A drop in air temperature can quickly turn the shallow water of impoundments cold enough to stun small fishes unless they can reach the warmer, deeper water of the bordering canals. Foresters terns, Caspian terns and winter gulls often congregate over schools of these cold-stunned fishes, diving into them or picking them off the surface as they struggle to survive. This occasional largess of easy-to-catch fish seldom benefits that other notable fish-eating bird, the osprey. By winter, most of the ACE Basin's nesting ospreys have migrated to Central and South America or at least have moved as far south as Florida to find enough fish on which to survive. In very cold weather, a skim of ice may form in the quiet corners of low-salinity impoundments, but a few days or more of normal winter weather can warm these shallow waters as quickly as the cold weather froze them. Typically, ACE Basin winters suffer only brief cold spells with short-term impacts, although the potential for a long spell of atypically cold weather with all its consequences always exists.

When a few days of rain that leave standing water in ditches and low spots follow mild winter weather, the uplands erupt in a cacophony of nocturnal sound, the breeding calls of several species of tiny chorus frogs. These very vocal members of the tree frog family, none more than an inch and a half in length, seldom climb, preferring to remain in low vegetation. Outside the breeding season, which lasts from November to March, they go completely unnoticed. On a mild mid-January evening, I roamed the dirt roads of Donnelley to listen to frogs in full voice. The sun had just settled below the horizon, leaving the treetops dark against the gold-tinted clouds when I first heard the rapid tapping call of an ornate chorus frog from an inundated firebreak. Then I picked out the rasping short trill of what I identified as a Brimley's chorus frog. Joining it, a southern chorus frog began a sort of musical ratchet, similar to the sound of a thumb raked across the teeth of a comb. Then came the louder "gick, gick, gick" of a southern cricket frog. All these calls arose from the same spot of low, wet vegetation although I saw none of these vocal little frogs just a few steps away.

As the twilight deepened, spring peepers took over, drowning out most of the other frogs with their high-pitched, endlessly repeated single "peep," slightly slurred at the end. At the flooded corner of a fallow field, the congregated peepers became absolutely deafening, almost painful to the ears. Better named "winter peepers" in the South, these plain brown chorus frogs, marked with a darker *X* on their back, breed throughout the winter in the ACE Basin and, judging by sound, seem to far outnumber the other native chorus frogs. Only the male frogs call as they attempt to attract females for breeding, and a male peeper's success in attracting a female depends on how loud and fast he calls. The females attach strings of fertilized eggs to vegetation in quiet pools of standing water. The eggs hatch in a few days to two weeks, and the resulting tadpoles take forty-five to sixty days to become adult frogs.

By full dark, the incessant calls of peepers and, when I could pick them out, the other chorus frogs projected loudly from any section of pinewoods with isolated patches of standing water. Interestingly, a drier hardwood ridge remained all but silent. Where the road crossed an old rice field reserve, I heard just a single peeper. Along the grassy edge of a fifty-acre impoundment, I heard only crickets. Chorus frogs avoid permanent bodies of water that support fish, many species of which prey heavily on tadpoles. Peepers and their kin seem to know that eggs deposited in permanent bodies of water have little chance of survival once they hatch into tadpoles. So in a typically wet winter, low spots in the more normally dry pinewoods hold much of the casual water that offers the best breeding habitat for these frogs.

Should a cold spell interrupt the breeding frogs, they simply burrow into the mud to wait for warmer weather. In severe cold, peepers, which range all across eastern North America well into Canada, can produce glucose, which acts as an antifreeze to prevent ice crystals from forming in their bodies, surviving and quickly recovering even after half their body fluid has frozen. Drought more than cold probably limits the success of all these chorus frogs. The low spots where these frogs breed have to remain flooded long enough for the tadpoles to turn into frogs ready to move onto dry land. During a late winter and early spring with little rainfall, the ephemeral pools and flooded ditches can dry up completely, dooming the developing tadpoles. However, in most years, enough peepers and their kin survive in at least a few wet spots to disperse across the uplands, where they wait for the rains of the following winter to start the cycle all over again.

A couple of days with full moon tides and onshore winds reshaped Townsend Inlet at the south end of Botany Bay beach. Just ankle deep at low tide a month earlier, it now appeared at least waist deep as it drained the marsh in a pronounced *S* curve. The recent high tides had also left a slender ribbon of flotsam all along the upper beach. A few days of heavier surf had dislodged all manner of creatures from the ocean floor and pushed them high onto the sand. Dozens of cast-off shells of young horseshoe crabs, left behind as they molted, dominated parts of this rack line. All these shells had a width of four to five inches, suggesting they came from perhaps one-year-old horseshoe crabs, still living close to shore. As these animals grow, they move to deeper water, finally becoming mature at an age of ten years. Scattered among this rack of worn oyster shells and decaying cord grass lay a few bright-yellow sea whips, branched coral resembling plants more than animals. The waves had also broken loose finger sponges, some still bright orange-red, others faded in death to a dull gray. The debris also contained a few pink blobs the size of my hand. Called sea pork, these pieces of colonial tunicates, or sea squirts, break off and wash ashore looking like chunks of raw meat until they, too, fade to nondescript beige. The rack line also included a couple of whelk egg cases—strings of whitish disks, each about the size of a quarter. The sharp edges on the disks suggested these came from channeled whelks, not the

Washed shells litter the rack line on the beach at Botany Bay Plantation WMA. *Pete Laurie.*

similar knobbed whelk, both common marine snails in South Carolina's near shore waters. Winter northeasters, even rather mild ones, can deposit onto the beach a sample of the great variety of the fascinating and diverse marine life that thrives just beyond the breakers.

On a cold, misty winter morning with just enough daylight to make out shapes in the gray landscape I walked Fishburne Bank, in the old rice field complex at Donnelley WMA. To the left, the salt marshes of the upper Chehaw River stretched toward a faint hint of daylight on the eastern horizon. On the right, I passed several brackish impoundments with still, dark waters and emergent vegetation shrouded in a thin fog. The indignant squawks of great blue herons and great egrets as they took flight mixed with the sharp "kik, kik, kik" of a Virginia rail deep in a stand of giant cordgrass. A muted quacking suggested unseen shovelers had already awoken and begun tipping up to reach the submerged widgeon grass. A great-horned owl hooted from the hardwoods on the far edge of the impoundment; then a second owl seemed to answer from the opposite direction. As the eastern sky grew brighter, a mockingbird awoke from a thicket of groundsel tree with a harsh screech and then flew to its nearby winter larder of bright-red berries on a Dahoon holly, an uncommon ACE Basin shrub. The thin chips of cardinals, still hidden in dense cover, signaled approaching daylight and inspired a Carolina wren to announce the dawn with a cheery, "Cheeseburger, cheeseburger, cheeseburger."

A week later, on the next-to-last duck hunt in late January at Bear Island WMA, hunters enjoyed as much success as earlier in the season, with sixteen hunters taking seventy-one birds of seven species. After picking up the hunters, Ross and I drove around a five-hundred-acre field not hunted that morning, the same field where, in November, Christy Hand and I had seen the many rails during the mowing and burning process. The now flooded field showed the dramatic results of those management practices. As we slowly drove the dikes circling the field, ducks got up in clouds, with many more staying on the water as far as we could see with binoculars. Mostly pintails and gadwall, with some shovelers mixed in, these birds feasted on the abundant crop of red root that Ross had learned how to grow successfully over the years. Back in May, he had flooded the field for about seven weeks to kill most other vegetation and then drained it and kept it dry all through the summer and fall. With little competition, the red root had flourished, and once mowing and burning removed the cover vegetation, the ducks needed only a few inches of water to float them within easy reach of the succulent roots.

We could only guess at the number of waterfowl that dotted the water surface and leapt into the air in huge, elongated flocks as the sharp quack of gadwall mingled with the two-note whistle of pintails. At one corner, a deer flushed from a small hummock of trees and splashed across the shallow water followed

Freshwater impoundments at Bear Island WMA attract thousands of gadwall, pintails and shovelers and many other waterfowl species during the winter. *Pete Laurie.*

by a second deer as they raced toward the cover of a larger wooded island. The ducks, very wary of our pickup truck, paid little heed to the nonthreatening deer galloping through their midst. We finally agreed on an estimate of fifteen thousand birds in this one pond, a dozen times the number of ducks that hunters usually take at Bear Island during the entire two-month season. The well-fed ducks that we saw by the thousands would leave Bear Island in another month or so in good health for the long flight to the northern breeding grounds and ready for a successful nesting season.

On our way back to the check station, we saw a flock of about fifteen avocets flying in tight formation over another pond. One of the largest and most graceful of the shorebirds, avocets, sharply white with black accents at this time of year, have increased in numbers throughout the ACE Basin during recent winters. Avocets nest on the western plains and fifty years ago only rarely wandered east of the Mississippi. However, like white pelicans, they now regularly winter on the southeastern coast and, for the last few years, have become common at Bear Island. With perhaps the longest legs relative to body size of any bird, avocets often feed in close ranks as they stride through the shallow impoundments sweeping their long, upturned bills from side to side in search of invertebrates. In deeper water, they can swim, tipping up to reach the bottom quite like ducks, and can even dive. Avocets represent another western species that has increased its winter range to include the extensive and productive wetlands of the ACE as such habitat has increasingly vanished in other areas due to coastal development and a rising demand for water, both for drinking and irrigation.

By late January, American shad have begun their spawning run up ACE Basin rivers, greatly preferring the much longer Edisto, which has supported a small, seasonal commercial fishery for shad probably since colonial times. Silvery on their sides with bluish-green backs, most spawning shad weigh about five pounds, the roes larger than the bucks. An anadramous species, shad spend most of their lives in the Atlantic Ocean. Each winter, at the age of four or five, shad leave the ocean and surge up coastal rivers, first into the James River in Florida, where they spawn in early January. As winter proceeds and gradually turns toward spring, American shad make spawning runs in other coastal rivers, moving farther north as waters in each river warm to fifty-five to sixty degrees until they finally reach the St. Lawrence River by June. South of Hatteras, shad spawn once and then die while north of Hatteras, this same species returns to the ocean after spawning and may spawn again in subsequent seasons. Females produce as many as 600,000 eggs, which float downstream, hatching in three to ten days. Juvenile shad remain in the river for about a month before entering the ocean.

With the demand for their oily flesh diminished and even shad roe, once considered a delicacy, now having lost much of its popularity, only a few hardy shad fishermen still drift gill nets each winter in the Edisto, with greater fishing effort farther north in the Santee and Waccamaw Rivers. Throughout their range, shad have declined in the past seventy-five years due to overfishing and the construction of dams that block access to spawning areas on many East Coast rivers. The Edisto remains one of the longest undammed rivers on the Atlantic coast and still provides spawning areas for this once abundant fish.

By early February, with the days now noticeable longer, chickasaw plums, among the earliest of bloomers, have erupted into rows of tiny white flowers along zigzag branches still bare of leaves. This small native shrub often forms dense thickets providing cover for bobwhites, rabbits and many other species. The yellowish-red fruit, ripe in late spring, provides food for a variety of birds and mammals. In another sign of approaching spring, the tiny blooms of red cedar emit clouds of yellow-green pollen on the slightest breeze. Male cardinals begin their cheery breeding song early on the still chilly mornings, and common yellow throats call "whitchy, whitchy, whitchy" from the cattails. In the hardwood understory, red bud trees, always among the first spring bloomers, suddenly turn bright pink.

One afternoon, I watched an adult eagle gliding slowly just above the brown vegetation along the edge of an impoundment. Abruptly, it dropped into the panic grass and disappeared from view. A minute or two later, it rose back into the air and, with a few powerful wing strokes, flew quickly toward the tree line. I could see something rather small and greenish dangling from its talons—perhaps the legs of a sora rail. Immediately, from high overhead, an immature eagle went into a steep dive, its wings folded as it hurled toward the other bird, which wheeled and began to climb. Then a second immature eagle joined the pursuit followed by a third, all hoping to force the adult to drop its prize so that one of them could grab it in midair. The adult, slowed by its burden, dodged and whirled, managing to elude its three pursuers until it gained the dense top of a loblolly pine. The younger birds peeled off and climbed higher but seemed to keep an eye on the adult, now almost hidden from view. I noticed the unmistakable dark mass of a relatively small eagle nest just a few trees away. Seen through binoculars, a tiny white patch just above the rim of the nest suggested a bird sitting on eggs. And indeed, this eagle, perhaps the mate of the first bird, abruptly stood up in the nest and then dropped down behind the pines and vanished. Eagles lay eggs from late November to early January, and with an incubation period of thirty-five days, a bird still sitting on eggs the first week of February seemed only a little late. The younger eagles had perhaps interrupted the adult in the process of bringing food to its mate.

With the end of waterfowl season for another year, small game hunters descended on the ACE Basin's state wildlife management areas for the remainder of February. On the first day of these small game hunts, more than a dozen rabbit hunters with scores of beagles took to the open fields and marshy edges of Bear Island. They sought not the cottontail rabbit so common across much of North America but the less well-known marsh rabbit. About the size of a cottontail, marsh rabbits live a largely nocturnal existence; people seldom see them except at dawn and dusk. With shorter ears, they lack the showy white tail and white feet of their better-known cousins and scamper more than hop, staying close to marshy habitats. Excellent swimmers, they often take to the water to escape predators, of which they have many. Hawks, owls, foxes, bobcats, alligators and snakes all relish marsh rabbits. Like most of their kin, they compensate for heavy predation by reproducing prolifically. Female marsh rabbits bear litters of three to five and can produce five or six litters annually. The wet soil of their environment does not lend itself to burrows, so they nest directly in the grass. They consume a variety of vegetation, including cattails, rushes, duck potato, pennywort, water hyacinth, blackberries and woody twigs. The little beagles flushed out very few marsh rabbits the first couple days of the hunt, but the hunters shrugged off their lack of success as just a down year for marsh rabbits, well known for cyclical swings in population.

Early one morning in mid-February, four of us, along with an experienced, well-trained dog named Dee, embarked on a different type of hunt: a late season squirrel hunt in the Salkehatchie Swamp. As the winter swamp came to life slowly with the dawn, the whistling of unseen wood ducks getting up among the buttressed tree trunks in the flooded sloughs mixed with the spring song of cardinals and the quiet "chuck" of a hermit thrush. A single querulous "wah?" of a distant barred owl punctuated a scattered cawing of a few crows passing above the tall oaks and tupelos. Heavy rains weeks ago had earlier pushed the Salkehatchie out of its meandering channel, covering the forest floor to a depth of a foot in most places. Now, however, the river had retreated back into its main channel, the swift current flowing darkly as it gurgled among the swaying willows, spinning little eddies along the bank.

As we moved to slightly higher but still regularly flooded portions of the swamp, the green twigs of the abundant high-bush blueberries sported reddish-pink buds, a few of which had already opened into small, drooping white flowers. By spring, these blueberries would provide an important food source for a variety of birds as well as possums, raccoons and many other species. From the edge of a swamp road, a woodcock jumped from the broom sedge and flew straight away from us, its short, rounded wings whistling as it paralleled the road at a height of six feet before abruptly veering off into the hardwoods. As its name implies, this short-necked member of the sandpiper family lives not along the shore but in wooded swamps and moist edges, where it probes with its long bill for earthworms and grubs. We thought ourselves fortunate to catch a glimpse of this primarily nocturnal bird during daylight, although a few hours later we flushed a second one. Woodcocks inhabit the ACE Basin's wooded swamps and their edges throughout the year, nesting in late February through March. During the winter, an influx of northern birds increases the local population.

Where a small drain flowed slowly through a pipe under the road, we noticed where beavers had peeled the bark from the base of several small trees, although we saw no beavers, another primarily nocturnal species. Beavers maintain a small population in scattered areas of the upper ACE Basin, sometimes causing timber damage by damming off and permanently

Well camouflaged on the forest floor, woodcocks often allow close approach before they flush. *Phillip Jones.*

flooding wooded areas. A pile of dark scat infused with hair we attributed to a coyote, also primarily nocturnal. The piercing, repeated cries of a red-shouldered hawk rang across the treetops as two birds dove and swooped at each other in perhaps a courtship display for this early nesting hawk that thrives in forested wetlands, preying on frogs, small snakes, skinks and crayfish. Meanwhile, the vocal wood ducks, in pairs and small groups, continued to fly back and forth above the treetops. Much of the winter woods, however, remained typically devoid of birdlife until we came upon a row of invasive tallow trees at a bend in one of the access roads. Here, feeding on the last of the popcorn berries, we watched a robin, several hermit thrushes and a pair of downy woodpeckers, along with a flicker and a white-eyed vireo. A couple of chickadees, yellow-rumped warblers and ruby-crowned kinglets joined them, all searching for insect eggs and pupae. More interestingly, a winter wren hopped about exposed tree roots along a drainage ditch. The bird's dark plumage and tiny upright tail identified it from the more common house wren, both winter visitors to the ACE Basin.

We spent most of the day tramping the bottomland hardwoods, interspersed with a few large loblolly and shortleaf pines growing here and there. We saw lots of squirrel nests and plenty of gnawed pinecones but no squirrels as the afternoon wore on. Dee, a mountain cur according to her owner, worked hard, ranging far ahead of us and then circling back, but never once barked to indicate she had found a fresh scent. The squirrels appeared quite content to stay in their nests and tree hollows on that particular day, although we never determined why. Nearing the river at one point, we came to a small spinoff stream flowing swiftly in the opposite direction as it curved around cypress trunks and knees into a deeper slough. Just eight to ten inches deep, the tannic water slid smoothly across the white bottom sand next to an ancient red maple, its bark pockmarked with thousands of old sapsucker holes in broken, horizontal rows. A flock of five or six golden-crowned kinglets searched among the tree's bare branches. A treetop bird, the golden-crowned kinglet occurs much less commonly in the ACE Basin than does its more abundant relative the rudy-crowned kinglet, a bird of the mid-story.

Finally, late in the afternoon, with the light just beginning to fade from the overcast sky, we gave up on finding any squirrels and started the long trek back to our starting point at the river house. Just then, Dee opened up on the first squirrel of the day. That one dove into a hollow in a live oak, but in the next hour, as we walked back to the house, Dee treed four more squirrels, all of which we managed to secure, the last just before the light faded to the point that we could no longer see them, clinging motionless, high in the oaks. Apparently, the Salkehatchie's entire squirrel population had waited until the last hour of the day to become active. Squirrel season generally runs from October 1 to March 1, but this remote area of private land had probably received little hunting pressure so that the few squirrels we removed had little impact on the overall population. We had enjoyed an interesting day in the swamp and brought home enough squirrels for at least a small stew.

On the next-to-last day of an unusually cold and damp February, I helped Be Moore, a volunteer at Botany Bay Plantation Wildlife Management Area, check the property's thirty wood duck boxes. Winter still held firm, with a chilly breeze that swayed the Spanish moss draping the live oaks as we sloshed through shallow puddles along the edge of a grassy slough. At each box, fashioned from rough-cut cypress, Moore mounted a small stepladder, unlatched the box's side door and gingerly swung it open. Most boxes contained nothing more than a three-inch layer of the fresh cedar shavings placed there a month earlier in preparation for the nesting season. In one box, a hunkered-down gray phase screech owl blinked at us without interest, never stirring from the shavings. In nine of the boxes, however, the opening of the door startled a sitting wood duck hen that with great thrashing of wing feathers bolted through the entrance hole and sped across the wetland with an excited "wheek, wheek, wheek." Moore then quickly counted the

A hen wood duck exits a nest box at Botany Bay Plantation WMA. *Phillip Jones.*

eggs and closed up the box, and we retreated out of sight to encourage the hen's prompt return. The clutches numbered ten to eighteen eggs, the latter in excess of a normal wood duck clutch of twelve or thirteen, suggesting that more than one hen might have "dumped" eggs in that box. The birds usually abandon such dump nests before the eggs hatch. Of the boxes that contained eggs, most bordered the freshwater portion of the slough and the edge of a small pond, also fresh. Of the boxes we checked along the slightly brackish portion of the slough, only one held a clutch of eggs, suggesting that, at Botany Bay at least, wood ducks can tolerate some salinity but much prefer fresh water.

Hens in the box at midday with numerous eggs indicated that these birds had completed a clutch and had started to incubate the eggs, a process that requires about thirty days. So while the migratory winter ducks—gadwall, widgeon, pintail, shoveler and all the rest—still lingered throughout the ACE Basin, the locally nesting wood ducks, not content to wait for spring, had already started a new generation. By the time the ducklings hatch and jump from the boxes, warmer weather should produce the insects that will nourish them for the couple of months before they can fly.

By noon, as we checked the last box, Moore and I had shed our heavy jackets. Winter had reached its last gasp, but as the nesting wood ducks showed us, life in the ACE Basin continued on, as the end of one season simply marked the beginning of another.

BIBLIOGRAPHY

Conant, Roger, and Joseph T. Collins. *Reptiles and Amphibians, Eastern/Central North America.* 3rd ed. Boston: Houghton Mifflin, 1998.

Daniels, Jared C. *Butterflies of the Carolinas.* Cambridge, MN: Adventure Publications, 2003.

DeVoe, M. Richard, and Douglas S. Baughman. *South Carolina Coastal Wetland Impoundments: Ecological Characterization, Management, Status and Use.* Charleston: South Carolina Sea Grant, 1987.

Earley, Lawrence S. *Looking for Longleaf.* Chapel Hill: University of North Carolina Press, 2004.

Laurie, Pete, and W. David Chamberlain. *The South Carolina Aquarium Guide to Aquatic Habitats of South Carolina.* Columbia: University of South Carolina Press, 2003.

Peterson, Roger Tory. *Birds of Eastern and Central North America.* 5th ed. Boston: Houghton Mifflin, 2002.

Porcher, Richard D. *Wildflowers of the Carolina Lowcountry and Lower Pee Dee.* Columbia: University of South Carolina Press, 1995.

BIBLIOGRAPHY

Porcher, Richard Dwight, and Douglas Alan Raynor. *A Guide to the Wildflowers of South Carolina*. Columbia: University of South Carolina Press, 2001.

Rohde, Fred C., Rudolf G. Arndt, David G. Lindquist and James F. Parnell. *Freshwater Fishes of the Carolinas, Virginia, Maryland, and Delaware*. Chapel Hill: University of North Carolina Press, 1994.

Sprunt, Alexander, Jr., and E. Burnham Chamberlain. *South Carolina Bird Life*. Columbia: University of South Carolina Press, 1949.

Terres, John K. *The Audubon Society Encyclopedia of North American Birds*. New York: Alfred A. Knopf, 1980.

Tiner, Ralph W. *Field Guide to Coastal Wetland Plants of the Southeastern United States*. Amherst: University of Massachusetts Press, 1993.

INDEX

A

ACE Basin National Estuarine Research
    Reserve 11, 25, 67, 133
ACE Basin Project 3, 7, 9, 10, 12, 14,
    15, 117, 159
Ace Basin Task Force 9, 13, 15, 93
alligators 22, 28, 42, 45, 77, 78, 79,
    132, 136, 144
American holly 25, 131, 133
American oystercatchers 49
American robins 105, 131, 132, 134,
    137, 146
American shad 23, 54, 143
anhingas 42, 43, 65, 112
armadillos 102, 130, 136
Ashe Island 11
Ashepoo Plantation 9, 12
Ashepoo River 7, 12, 15, 51, 63, 64,
    68, 72, 73, 85, 133
avocets 28, 35, 142

B

Bachman's sparrows 39
bald cypress 20, 22, 23, 102

bald eagles 22, 29, 62, 78, 99, 112,
    116, 126, 127
barn owls 98
beach 14, 16, 17, 48, 49, 50, 51, 68,
    70, 73, 74, 75, 76, 86, 87, 104,
    105, 128, 129, 130, 139, 140
Bear Island Wildlife Management Area
    8, 9, 28, 29, 31, 32, 35, 46, 61,
    62, 63, 64, 67, 75, 89, 91, 97,
    98, 106, 107, 108, 109, 112,
    113, 117, 118, 119, 120, 127,
    133, 141, 142, 144
Beaufort County 12, 81
Beet Island 11
Bennetts Point Road 12, 35, 67, 81, 133
Big Island 11
black-bellied whistling duck 45, 93
black ducks 45
black gum 23, 79, 88
black needle rush 19, 22
black rails 106, 107
blazing stars 89, 99, 101
blue crabs 47, 60, 68, 70, 97
blue-winged teals 28, 91, 120
bobcats 56, 58, 85, 89, 97, 119, 144
bob-o-links 46

INDEX

Bonny Hall Club 10
Botany Bay Wildlife Management Area
    13, 14, 15, 33, 48, 49, 51, 75,
    76, 86, 87, 98, 99, 113, 128,
    139, 140, 147, 148
brown shrimp 47, 60
Buzzard Island 11

C

canebreak 44
Carolina wrens 27, 38, 141
Charleston County 10, 72, 82
Cheeha-Combahee 10
chipping sparrows 40, 134
chorus frogs 40, 136, 138, 139
Christmas Bird Count 133, 136
chuck-will's-widows 36
clapper rails 68
Colleton County 7, 10
Combahee River 7, 8, 10, 12, 15, 36,
    40, 51, 57, 63, 72, 81, 82, 93,
    122, 124, 126, 133
common gallinules 54
controlled burn 30, 31, 32, 37, 40, 54, 81
Cooper's hawks 54, 78, 82, 119
coots 112, 118, 127, 136
copperheads 94
cottonmouths 79, 94
cowbirds 40
coyotes 89, 102, 113, 146

D

Dahoon holly 141
dissolved oxygen 18, 47, 60, 68, 70,
    76, 78
Donnelley, Dorothy 9, 12
Donnelley, Gaylord 9, 12
Donnelley Wildlife Management Area
    12, 27, 42, 78
double-crested cormorants 112
dowitchers 29, 30, 103
drought 23, 40, 42, 53, 54, 71, 139
Ducks Unlimited 8, 9, 12

dunlins 128
DuPont, Eugene 12
dwarf spike rush 22, 60, 61, 89, 91

E

Edisto River 7, 8, 10, 11, 12, 13, 14,
    15, 17, 18, 53, 54, 63, 67, 68,
    70, 71, 72, 73, 76, 88, 89, 91,
    100, 104, 106, 112, 143
estuary 18, 19, 20, 104

F

fiddler crabs 19, 48, 51, 70, 86
Fields Point 36, 95, 114
fox squirrels 102

G

gadwall 28, 110, 119, 120, 135, 136,
    141, 142, 148
golden canna lily 29, 56
golden silk spiders 92
gray squirrels 88, 102
great egrets 43, 77, 112, 141
greater yellowlegs 28, 29
great-horned owls 56, 113, 116,
    119, 141
green-winged teals 136
Grove Plantation 10, 11

H

hemp sesbania 92, 111, 112
hermit thrushes 105, 136, 145, 146
Hollings ACE Basin National Wildlife
    Refuge 10, 11, 57, 72, 88, 133
Hollings, Ernest F. 10
house wrens 146
hunting
    deer 80, 81, 113
    squirrel 145, 147
    waterfowl 7, 8, 21, 45, 117, 120, 141

INDEX

I

impoundment 31, 35, 60, 61, 62, 64, 102, 106, 110, 118, 134, 138, 141, 144
indigo buntings 67

L

Lane, Hugh, Sr. 9
Lavington Plantation 12
least sandpipers 29, 86, 103
leopard frogs 28, 79
lesser yellowlegs 30
little blue herons 28, 66, 94
live oak 16, 25, 39, 40, 49, 54, 67, 72, 79, 84, 88, 89, 91, 98, 99, 102, 119, 147
loblolly pine 24, 27, 37, 43, 57, 88, 94, 102, 116, 126, 132, 134, 144, 146
longleaf pine 35, 36, 37, 38, 57, 116, 122, 124, 125
Lowcountry Open Land Trust 13

M

marbled godwits 74, 75, 104
marsh hens 82, 96, 97
marsh rabbits 144, 145
marsh wrens 33, 50, 112
Mary's Island Plantation 11
Mathewes Canal 63, 91, 110
McKenzie, Michael D. 13
MeadWestvaco 13
minks 96, 97
mockingbirds 105, 141
Morgan Island 11
mottled ducks 45, 46, 91, 93, 120
Murdock, Nora 8

N

National Wild Turkey Federation 12
Nature Conservancy, The 9, 10
Nemours Plantation 12, 55, 122, 123, 126

Norfolk Southern Railroad 13
northern pintails 110, 119, 120, 136, 141, 142, 149
northern shovelers 28, 112, 119, 120, 141, 142, 149
no-see-ums 35

O

Orangeburg 13
ospreys 22
Otter Island 11, 15, 25, 73, 76, 103, 104, 128
otters 22, 48, 50, 96, 104

P

painted buntings 67, 72, 99
palm warblers 91
panic grass 16, 22, 89, 106, 110, 144
parula warblers 32, 39, 91
Pepper, Margaret 14
pignut hickory 37
pileated woodpeckers 94
Pine Island 11, 25, 73, 76, 103, 104, 128
pine warblers 37, 134
prothonotary warblers 51, 85

R

raccoons 22, 42, 45, 50, 58, 79, 81, 96, 97, 104, 124, 145
rainfall 18, 20, 40, 42, 47, 52, 60, 62, 71, 72, 78, 79, 95, 113, 120, 139
rattlebox 89
rattle bush 92
red-bellied woodpeckers 37, 51, 131
redbreasts 52, 53, 54, 85, 115
red-cockaded woodpeckers 122, 123, 124, 125, 126, 137
red knot 17, 103, 128
red maple 27, 113, 116
red root 22, 106, 110, 141
red-shouldered hawks 78, 117, 146
red-tailed hawks 37, 78, 94, 137

INDEX

red-winged blackbirds 67, 92, 137
rice
  field 7, 21, 28, 29, 42, 57, 62, 63, 76,
      88, 126, 138, 141
    plantation 12, 21, 45, 81, 117
    planters 7, 20, 21, 40, 42, 46, 62, 63, 72
    reserve 28, 45, 93
rice field trunk 29, 62, 159
roseate spoonbills 62, 77, 99, 119
rough-winged swallows 67, 112
ruddy ducks 112, 120
rufous-sided towhees 27, 40

S

salinity 18, 22, 51, 52, 60, 61, 62, 68,
    70, 72, 73, 89, 115, 137, 148
Salkehatchie Swamp 22, 93, 95, 145
salt marsh 10, 16, 19, 22, 30, 47, 48,
    49, 59, 61, 62, 72, 74, 82, 90,
    97, 98, 99, 102, 103, 104, 105
salt marsh cord grass 19
Sampson Island 9, 31
sea ox-eye 49, 74, 104
sedge wrens 111, 135
shortleaf pine 53, 124, 146
sora rails 29, 106, 107, 108, 134, 144
South Carolina Department of Natural
    Resources 4, 8, 11, 13, 14, 20,
    42, 45, 48, 49, 50, 53, 68, 73,
    98, 106, 127, 128, 137, 159, 160
southern red oak 27, 37
South Williman Island 11
spartina 19, 48, 62, 69, 70, 72, 73, 82,
    86, 95, 96, 97, 98, 99, 105, 128
spotted sandpipers 82
Springfield Marsh 8, 91
spring peeper 136, 138
St. Helena Sound 10, 11, 17, 20, 59,
    68, 100, 104
stilt sandpipers 30
summer tanagers 35, 37, 43, 53, 58, 88
swamp 20, 23, 27, 33, 39, 45, 85, 94,
    95, 107, 111, 115, 132, 145, 147
swamp chestnut oak 94

swamp sparrows 107, 111

T

tree frogs 138
tree swallows 112, 119
tundra swans 28, 118
Turner, Ted 9

U

upland 9, 30, 80, 81, 130, 134, 135, 137
U.S. Army Corps of Engineers 12
U.S. Fish and Wildlife Service 8, 10,
    120, 122
U.S. Highway 17 12, 13, 57, 63, 82
U.S. Highway 17A 13

V

velvet ants 90, 91
Virginia rails 107, 108, 141

W

Warren Island 11
wax myrtle 25, 31, 112
wetland management 22, 29, 30, 61,
    62, 64, 81, 89, 120, 136, 141
whimbrels 48, 69, 86
white ibises 85, 112, 115, 118, 135
white pelicans 28, 62, 77, 118, 134, 142
white shrimp 47, 59, 60, 70, 86, 137
white-tailed deer 22, 81
white-throated sparrows 115, 131, 135
widgeon 22, 60, 61, 62, 89, 91, 110,
    119, 120, 135, 141, 149
widgeon grass 22, 60, 61, 62, 89, 91,
    119, 135, 141
wild azalea 35
wild turkeys 33, 55
Wilson's plovers 49, 50
winter wrens 146
woodcocks 145
wood ducks 45, 93, 115, 116, 135, 145,
    146, 147, 148, 149
wood storks 42, 44, 54, 66

Y

yaupon holly 25, 82, 102
yellow-billed cuckoos 51, 54
yellow rails 107, 108
yellow rat snakes 28
yellow-rumped warblers 28, 33, 131,
      134, 135, 137, 146
yellow-throated warblers 27, 31, 39,
      43, 53, 131, 132

ABOUT THE AUTHOR
AND PHOTOGRAPHER

A native of Pennsylvania, Pete Laurie graduated from Lehigh University in 1968 with a bachelor of arts in natural science. An air force veteran, he worked for the South Carolina Department of Natural Resources for twenty-seven years as a writer and photographer, retiring in 1999. Laurie has worked in and written about the ACE Basin Project since its inception in 1988. He has served as co-editor of the ACE Basin newsletter, assisted in the production of special publications, written numerous magazine stories, led bird-watching groups and built rice field trunks. He also co-authored *The South Carolina Aquarium Guide to Aquatic Habitats of South Carolina.* Laurie has an extensive knowledge of coastal ecology and a lifelong interest in birds. He currently works as a freelance magazine writer, specializing in natural history subjects.

ABOUT THE AUTHOR AND PHOTOGRAPHER

Phillip Jones has photographed wildlife for forty-three years as a staff photographer for the South Carolina Department of Natural Resources. Now retired, he continues as a freelance photographer for *South Carolina Wildlife* magazine. A native of Columbia, South Carolina, and a navy veteran, Jones also recently retired from the South Carolina National Guard after more than forty-three years of service.

Phillip Jones and Pete Laurie have worked together on magazine assignments for more than four decades.